Meredith Levy   Diana Goodey

Messages

Teacher's Book

1

CAMBRIDGE
UNIVERSITY PRESS

CAMBRIDGE UNIVERSITY PRESS
Cambridge, New York, Melbourne, Madrid, Cape Town, Singapore, São Paulo

Cambridge University Press
The Edinburgh Building, Cambridge CB2 2RU, UK

www.cambridge.org
Information on this title: www.cambridge.org/9780521614252

First published 2005

Printed in the United Kingdom at the University Press, Cambridge

A catalogue record for this book is available from the British Library

ISBN-13 978-0-521-61425-2 Teacher's Book
ISBN-10 0-521-61425-2 Teacher's Book

ISBN-13 978-0-521-54707-9 Student's Book
ISBN-10 0-521-54707-5 Student's Book

ISBN-13 978-0-521-54708-6 Workbook with Audio CD
ISBN-10 0-521-54708-3 Workbook with Audio CD

ISBN-13 978-0-521-61426-9 Teacher's Resource Pack
ISBN-10 0-521-61426-0 Teacher's Resource Pack

ISBN-13 978-0-521-61427-6 Class Cassettes
ISBN-10 0-521-61427-9 Class Cassettes

ISBN-13 978-0-521-61428-3 Class Audio CDs
ISBN-10 0-521-61428-7 Class Audio CDs

Contents

Map of the Student's Book   4

Introduction   6

Teacher's notes and keys

Module 1 Facts

1 What do you remember?   10
2 Are you ready?   16
Module 1 Review   23

Module 2 Things and people

3 What have you got?   26
4 Descriptions   33
Module 2 Review   40

Module 3 Daily life

5 My world   42
6 I'm usually late!   49
Module 3 Review   55

Module 4 Inside and outside

7 At home   58
8 Having fun   64
Module 4 Review   70

Module 5 Today and tomorrow

9 At the moment   72
10 Plans   79
Module 5 Review   85

Module 6 Looking back

11 About the past   87
12 Heroes   94
Module 6 Review   101

Games   103

Workbook key and tapescripts   104

Acknowledgements   112

	Grammar	Vocabulary and Pronunciation	Listening and Reading skills	Communicative tasks
Module 1 Facts — **Unit 1** What do you remember?	• Revision: *I'm, I live, I've got* • *He/She …, His/Her …* • Classroom language • *Can*: asking for permission and help	• Revision of known vocabulary • Numbers and dates • The alphabet • Things in the classroom	• Punctuation • Listen to and understand a song • Read a letter in English • *Life and culture*: Alphabet world	• Tell the class about yourself • Ask and answer questions about you and your friends • Talk to your teacher in English • Write a letter to an English friend
Unit 2 Are you ready?	• *Be:* affirmative, negative, questions, short answers • Questions with *What, Where, Who, When* • Singular and plural nouns	• Members of a band • Interests and activities • Countries and cities • Geography • *Rhythm drill:* word stress	• Read an email • Listen to an interview for a student survey • Listen to a radio quiz • *Life and culture:* The UK	• Ask for and give information • Write about an imaginary band • Describe your interests • Talk about cities and countries • Play a quiz game
Review	*Study skills:* Your coursebook *How's it going?:* Progress check *Coursework:* Facts about me			
Module 2 Things and people — **Unit 3** What have you got?	• *Have got* • *A, an, some, any* • Possessive *'s* • Possessive adjectives • *This/these, that/those*	• Everyday things • Families • *Rhythm drill:* plural nouns: /s/, /z/, /ɪz/	• Listen for specific information • Read an announcement • *Story: The Silent Powers* Chapter 1 • *Life and culture:* Collections	• Talk about possessions, and things you use at school • Say who something belongs to • Write a description of a family
Unit 4 Descriptions	• *What is/are … like?* • *Has got* • Adjectives	• Appearance and personality • The body • *I've got a headache/cold* • /h/ and links between words • Stress in sentences	• Read a 'Happiness Recipe' • Listen to personal descriptions • Listen to and understand a song • *Story: The Silent Powers* Chapter 2 • *Life and culture:* London	• Ask about and describe things • Write a 'Happiness recipe' • Describe people's appearance and personality • Say how you feel • Write about an imaginary person
Review	*Study skills:* Using a dictionary *How's it going?:* Progress check *Coursework:* Important things to me			
Module 3 Daily life — **Unit 5** My world	• Present simple: affirmative, negative, questions, short answers • Revision of question forms • *Wh-* questions	• Things you do regularly • Scary things • Verb + /s/, /z/, /ɪz/ • Stress and intonation in questions	• Read about British teenagers • Listen to and understand a song • *Story: The Silent Powers* Chapter 3 • *Life and culture:* Schools	• Describe things you do • Write about teenagers • Talk about fears, likes and dislikes • Write a questionnaire • Make a conversation about daily life
Unit 6 I'm usually late!	• Present simple + frequency adverbs • *Have + a meal,* etc.	• Food, drink and meals • The time • Daily routines • *Rhythm drill:* vowel sounds	• Read and listen to a questionnaire • Listen to a conversation about meals • Read a report about food in the UK • Listen to a description of someone's day • *Story: The Silent Powers* Chapter 4 • *Life and culture:* My name is Dion	• Describe your habits • Talk about things you eat and drink • Write a report about food • Ask for and tell the time • Describe daily routines
Review	*Study skills:* How do you learn? *How's it going?:* Progress check *Coursework:* A day in my life			

	Grammar	Vocabulary and Pronunciation	Listening and Reading skills	Communicative tasks
Module 4 Inside and outside				
Unit 7 At home	• *There is/are* • Uncountable nouns • Prepositions	• Homes • Things in a room • Food • *Rhythm drill:* stress in sentences	• Read a shopping list • Listen to a conversation in a supermarket • *Story: The Silent Powers* Chapter 5 • *Life and culture:* Homes in the UK	• Describe different homes • Write a description of your dream home • Ask about places and food • Write a 'disgusting recipe' • Describe a room
Unit 8 Having fun	• *Can* for ability and possibility • *I can see, I can hear* • *Must, mustn't* • Imperative	• Abilities • Places in a town • *Can* /æ/, *can't* /ɑː/, weak form of *can* /ə/	• Listen to and understand a song • Read a newspaper article • Read a poem • *Story: The Silent Powers* Chapter 6 • *Life and culture:* Stephen Hawking	• Talk about your abilities • Make a notice for a club • Describe things you can do in your town • Describe the sights and sounds around you • Tell people what to do • Write a short poem
Review	*Study skills:* Learning vocabulary *How's it going?:* Progress check *Coursework:* My neighbourhood			
Module 5 Today and tomorrow				
Unit 9 At the moment	• Present continuous: affirmative, negative, questions, short answers • Object pronouns	• Clothes • Football • *Rhythm drill: -ing* /ɪŋ/	• Listen to a football commentary • Read about the World Cup • Listen to a conversation at a football stadium • *Story: The Silent Powers* Chapter 7 • *Life and culture:* Sports fans	• Describe things in progress at the moment • Play a guessing game • Describe what you're wearing now, and what you usually wear
Unit 10 Plans	• Present continuous used for the future • Suggestions • The future with *going to*	• Future time expressions • The weather • Weak form of *to* /tə/ in *going to*	• Read a list of items in a café and a shop • Listen to and understand a song • Read a postcard • *Story: The Silent Powers* Chapter 8 • *Life and culture:* An exchange visit	• Talk about future arrangements • Make and reply to suggestions • Write a message to a friend • Describe plans and intentions • Talk about the weather • Write a holiday postcard
Review	*Study skills:* Parts of speech *How's it going?:* Progress check *Coursework:* My clothes			
Module 6 Looking back				
Unit 11 About the past	• Past simple of *be* and regular verbs: affirmative, *Wh-* questions	• Occupations • *Rhythm drill:* verbs + *-ed* /t/ /d/ /ɪd/	• Listen to a conversation with a ghost • Read dictionary definitions • *Story: The Silent Powers* Chapter 9 • *Life and culture:* From North to South	• Talk about people from the past • Play a quiz game • Write about an imaginary person's life • Describe your early childhood
Unit 12 Heroes	• Past simple: negatives, questions, short answers; irregular verbs	• Past time expressions • Words with the same vowel sound	• Listen to a list of events in the past • Read an advertisement • Listen to and understand a song • *Story: The Silent Powers* Chapter 10 • *Life and culture:* Quiz: The UK and the USA	• Describe things that happened in the past • Write a letter about an event in the past • Write a diary • Talk about your school year
Review	*Study skills:* Planning your learning *How's it going?:* Progress check *Coursework:* My life line			

• Grammar index • Communicative functions index • Wordlist • Spelling notes • Lexical sets and irregular verbs • Songs

Introduction

Welcome to *Messages*, a lower-secondary course providing **80–90 hours of classwork** per level. *Messages* is designed to meet the needs of you and your students by making both learning and teaching **simple and effective**. It has a **clearly structured** progression in both grammar and vocabulary, and a wealth of opportunities for students to practise the language they are learning.

We hope that students will find *Messages* an enjoyable, engaging course, with its clear signposting of aims, **interesting and motivating themes**, and a wide range of **rich resources**. Teachers will find it offers **practical**, **easy-to-use material** that can be adapted to **mixed-ability classes**. *Messages* 1 is designed for students who have studied English previously at primary level, but includes revision of all basic structures.

Course components

Student's Book
- Six modules of two units each
- Module opening pages
- Extra exercises page with KET-style activities
- Extra readings on Life and Culture
- Continuous story *The Silent Powers*
- Review sections at the end of every module, containing grammar and vocabulary summaries, consolidation exercises, study skills and a progress check
- Coursework
- Reference section that contains:
  - Grammar index
  - Communicative functions index
  - Wordlist
  - Spelling notes
  - Lexical sets
  - Song lyrics
  - Phonetic symbols

Workbook
- Full range of exercises, including more KET-style activities
- Extension activities for stronger learners
- Learning diary
- Comprehensive grammar notes
- CD with Workbook audio, pattern drills and animated tour of the Infoquests

Teacher's Book
- Step-by-step, easy-to-follow instructions
- Student's Book answers
- Background information on texts
- Guidelines for how and when to include supplementary material
- Ideas for language games in the classroom
- Tapescript for the Student's Book audio
- Workbook answer key

Teacher's Resource Pack
- Photocopiable activities:
  - Entry test
  - Communicative activities
  - Grammar worksheets
  - Module tests
  - Final test
- Pattern drills
- Teaching notes and answers

Audio CDs/Cassettes
- Student's Book audio
- Tests audio

Web material
- Infoquests at www.cambridge.org/elt/messages/infoquest
- Downloadable worksheets and Teacher's guides for Infoquests at www.cambridge.org/elt/messages/teacherquest
- Downloadable grammar worksheets for weaker learners at www.cambridge.org/elt/messages

About *Messages*

A sense of purpose and achievement

In *Messages*, there are three levels at which students focus on what they can do in English:
- The units are divided into three steps. The step begins with a description of the target language and the communicative task(s) (*Use what you know*) which students will be able to do, using that language. Each step takes students through a series of related activities, which lead them quickly from 'input' of new language to meaningful, communicative 'output'. Short, carefully prepared and guided tasks ensure that even weaker students can enjoy a sense of success.
- At the end of each module, students complete one part of a portfolio of personal information entitled 'All about me'. This is a continuous *Coursework* project, based on different aspects of the overall theme of the book (see below) and on the language of the preceding units. Language is recycled and revised in the modules themselves and in the reviews, tests and additional material.
- There is an overall purpose to each year's work. Each book has its own theme, exemplified in the six *Coursework* tasks. In Book 1, the theme is 'Everyday life' and, by the end of the year, students should be able to describe themselves, their interests and everyday lives in simple English.

Authentic and meaningful language learning

Although the language in *Messages* 1 is, of necessity, simple and controlled, it is as natural and realistic as possible, presented and practised in authentic contexts. Students will learn about their English-speaking counterparts, and about the world around them.

Active, responsible learners

In the units, students engage actively with the material and use a range of cognitive skills such as guessing, deducing, comparing, matching, sequencing. Students are asked to discover sentence patterns and grammar rules for themselves, to make their own exercises and to 'test a friend'. There are frequent opportunities for students to talk about themselves and their interests.

In the reviews, a series of exercises and tasks help learners to monitor what they can do. In *How's it going?* they make their own assessment of their grasp of the language points covered. This is reinforced when they complete the *Learning diary* in the Workbook.

Using *Messages* 1

You will find detailed suggestions for each activity in the unit notes that follow. In general:

Module openers

These two pages allow teachers to 'set the scene' for their students, concerning both the information and language content of what will come in the module itself. This helps to motivate students by creating interest and by showing them what they will be able to do by the end of the module.

The pages contain a selection of visuals from the coming units, a list of what students will study in the module and what they will be able to do at the end of it, and a brief matching exercise.

You may need to translate some of the language points for weaker classes, but encourage all classes to say as much as they can about the pictures before they do the matching exercise.

With stronger classes, you may want to ask students to identify which language point each of the sentences relates to, or to supply similar sentences.

Presentation

There is a wide variety of presentation texts and dialogues. They each present the new grammar point in a context which illustrates its concept and meaning, as well as providing plenty of natural examples of it.

Always begin by setting the scene (for example, by asking students to comment on the photos), so that learners can anticipate what they are about to hear.

In some cases, students listen first with their books closed (or the text covered). This will enable them to focus on the sounds of the language without being distracted – and sometimes confused – by its written equivalent.

Ask plenty of comprehension questions, and get students to repeat the key sentences. They should listen to/read the conversation/text at least twice during this phase of the lesson.

Key grammar

Key grammar activities follow on from the Presentations and focus on the language within them. Give students a few moments to look at the grammar box and reflect before they discuss and complete the examples and explanations orally.

Write the completed sentences on the board; students can then copy them into their notebooks. In some cases, students translate the examples and compare them with the mother tongue equivalent.

Practice

The controlled practice exercises which always follow Key grammar sections can be done orally with the whole class, and then individually in writing.

Students are often asked to then make their own 'exercise' and **Test a friend**. Look at the example in the book with the whole class first, adding further examples on the board if necessary. This is an excellent opportunity for students to focus actively on the new grammar and test their understanding. It also gives you a chance to monitor and deal with any difficulties they may have before you move on.

For additional oral practice, there is a set of **pattern drills** in the Teacher's Resource Pack, with the corresponding audio on the Workbook CD. Recommendations for when to use the pattern drills are made in the unit notes of the Teacher's Book. We suggest you play the complete drill through at least once, before pausing for the students to respond each time. You may prefer to do the drills yourself, without the recorded version.

Key vocabulary

These are mainly matching activities, many of them with a time limit. Most of the lexical groups include items which students should know from primary school, as well as some new words. Students can work alone or in pairs, and use their dictionaries for words they don't know.

The core vocabulary of each unit is practised further in the Workbook. Encourage students to start their own vocabulary notebooks and to record new vocabulary in them.

Key pronunciation

Messages 1 focuses on basic areas, such as stress in multi-syllable words, the pronunciation of final *-s*, weak forms, and stress and intonation in sentences.

Some of the pronunciation practice comes in the form of **rhythm drills** where students listen and then join in. The pronunciation activities are always linked to the language of the unit.

Speaking

Students are encouraged to repeat key vocabulary and the key sentences of each presentation. In addition, new language is practised in meaningful contexts that involve an element of creativity on the part of the learner, with an emphasis on moving from accuracy to fluency. Students create and practise simple four-line dialogues, make quiz questions, invent sentences about themselves, their friends and families, and their wider environment.

Speaking can also be encouraged by giving students the chance to act out rough or reduced versions of some of the presentation dialogues, and also to engage in **role plays**. The aim here should be to reproduce the situation rather than the original conversation word for word. Stronger students can work in groups and act a slightly different conversation.

Writing

Writing is introduced gradually and is always carefully guided. There is a variety of task types, from simple sentences to a postcard, a diary and a letter.

For longer writing tasks, encourage students to first write a rough draft, then read through and check their work before writing a final version. They could also check each others' work from time to time.

Use what you know

The **Use what you know** tasks at the end of each step enable students to use what they have learnt for an authentic, communicative purpose. Many of these tasks can be prepared in writing and then done orally, or vice versa. Students are always given examples to follow, and you will find a model answer where applicable in the notes that follow in this Teacher's Book.

Some of the tasks can be prepared in class and then done for **homework**.

Listening

Attention to receptive skills is vital in the early stages of learning English, so there is an emphasis on providing abundant, varied input.

Many learners find listening particularly difficult, so *Messages* 1 provides plenty of practice of this skill. Students will listen to the presentation texts and dialogues, and have the chance to read them at the same time, and there is also a specific listening task in each unit, covering a variety of different text types (for example, conversations, a radio quiz, an interview etc.). These may include language which is slightly beyond the students' productive level. However, they are not expected to understand or reproduce everything they have heard. You should focus on the key sentences only. Remember that learners may need to listen more than twice during these activities.

Songs

The six songs have been written as an integral part of the book – a musical form of listening comprehension. They can be used for:
- global comprehension (Unit 1)
- teaching and practising vocabulary (Unit 4)
- teaching and practising vocabulary and grammar (Units 5, 8, 10 and 12).

Once the specific work on the songs has been done, students may enjoy singing them! The words are given on page 144 of the Student's Book.

Reading

There is a short reading task in each unit, covering a range of text types, for example: a magazine article, an announcement, a report, an advertisement etc. Students will usually read the text once for 'gist' and then move on to more detailed questions. The texts develop reading strategies such as skimming and scanning.

Extra reading practice is provided through:
- an extra reading text with each unit, dealing with **Life and culture** in the English-speaking world.
- the story *The Silent Powers*, which begins in Unit 3. This provides an opportunity for reading for pleasure. Students' confidence will be greatly enhanced by the knowledge that they can read and understand a continuous story. Each chapter

of the story is accompanied by a puzzle in the Student's Book, while background information, comprehension questions and detailed suggestions for its exploitation are given in the Teacher's Book.

The listening and reading activities include a range of **KET text types**.

Consolidation and testing

At the end of each unit, there is a page of extra exercises on the language of the unit, providing practice of **KET-style tasks**.

At the end of every module, preceding work is pulled together in the **Review**. For each language point, students complete a task showing what they can do. This, together with the following vocabulary summary, prepares and leads them into the **Coursework** task.

There is a model each time, based on the character Jack, for you to study with the whole class. Individual coursework can then be done at home over a period of a couple of weeks or so. At the end of the year, the student's **Coursework** comprises a coherent and self-contained set of assignments, based on a clear model.

In addition, the Review section includes work on **study skills** to help students become more independent and effective learners, and a chance for students to assess their own progress.

Further consolidation of the language in the modules can be achieved through the **communicative activities** and **grammar worksheets** from the Teacher's Resource Pack, which should be done at the end of each unit when all the work has been covered, and through the accompanying **Infoquests** on the web (see below).

Students' progress can be more formally tested through the use of the **photocopiable module tests** in the Teacher's Resource Pack, which examine grammar, vocabulary, reading, writing, listening and speaking, often through KET-style activities. The audio for the listening element of the tests can be found on the class CDs/cassettes.

Workbook

Workbook activities should, in the main, be done for homework, though they can be prepared in class with weaker students if necessary, and you can also give stronger students the Extension exercises if they finish earlier than their classmates. Make sure you have covered the relevant part of the step before students begin the corresponding Workbook exercises.

At the end of the unit, students complete their **Learning diary**. The **Workbook answer key** can be found on pages 104–112 of the Teacher's Book.

Infoquests

Each module of the course is accompanied by an Infoquest, in which students are encouraged to find information on **specially designed websites** and to work co-operatively. The websites are housed at **http://www/cambridge.org/elt/messages/infoquest** and are designed to reinforce the language of each module, and should therefore be done at the end of the module.

Free **accompanying worksheets** and clear **Teacher's guides** can be found at
http://www/cambridge.org/elt/messages/teacherquest. You will need to complete a simple form to register and then get

access to these items, and will need to log in with your user name and password each time you want to use them.

Classroom management

Creating an 'English' atmosphere
Use every opportunity to bring 'the real world' into the classroom: maps, posters, magazines etc. Encourage students to look for examples of English 'text' outside the classroom: words from pop songs, instructions for a machine, English food packaging in a supermarket etc.

Use classroom instructions in English from the beginning, and get students to address you in English as much as possible.

Making good progress
A wide variety of task types ensures regular changes of pace and activity, with frequent opportunities for students to work at their own level. Work at a lively pace and have the courage to move on even though students may not have learnt everything in a lesson perfectly. Some of the activities include a time limit, to encourage students to work quickly and to introduce a 'game' element.

Dealing with classes of mixed ability
There are a large number of personalised and open-ended activities which allow students to respond in different ways, depending on their ability. The rubric **do at least ...** also enables students to work at their own level. Other activities (**If you have time. Try this!** and the **Extension** exercises in the Workbook) can also be used by pupils who finish early.

Try to make sure you involve all the students. For example, ask weaker students to suggest single words to describe a photo, while stronger students might think of a question to ask about it. When you ask a question, give everyone the chance to think of the answer before calling on individuals to do so. When doing individual repetition, ask stronger students first, but be careful not to make this too obvious by always varying the order, and who you call on.

Use the different skills of the students in as many ways as you can. The student who hates speaking may enjoy writing vocabulary on the board, while another student may be good at drawing, or making posters.

Try to build an atmosphere in which students communicate with you and with each other in a respectful, courteous and good-humoured manner. Never underestimate the importance of praise and encouragement: *That's great! Well done! Good!*

Explaining new words
New vocabulary which arises other than in the Key vocabulary section can be explained using visual aids such as your own set of flash cards, pictures on the blackboard, mime, contextualised examples or, if necessary, translation. Encourage students to guess the meaning of new words as well as using their dictionaries.

Controlled oral repetition
The key vocabulary and the key sentences can be reinforced through choral and individual repetition. This helps students 'get their tongues round' the sounds of the new language.

When asking a question, give everyone time to think of the answer before asking an individual student by name. When two or three individuals have responded, finish by getting the whole class to repeat.

Get students to ask as well as answer questions. Questions and answers can be drilled by dividing the class in two and getting the groups to take it in turns to ask and answer, before moving on to drilling with two individual students.

When drilling words or sentences, you can beat the stress of words and sentences with your hand to show where the main stress is – exaggerate slightly if necessary. You can also use your hand to show whether the sentence goes up or down at the end.

With long sentences, use 'back-chaining':
... half past ten.
... to bed at half past ten.
I usually go to bed at half past ten.

Pairwork
Getting students to work in pairs will greatly increase the amount of English spoken in the classroom, even if some students may use the mother tongue. Walk round and listen whilst students are speaking. Vary the pairings so that students do not always work with the same partner. Always give examples of what you want students to do and check that they understand the activity clearly.

Group work
Some of the activities in *Messages* 1 can be done in groups if you wish. Ensure first that everyone is clear about what they are doing, then monitor their work and don't let the activity drag on for too long. Use mixed-ability groups and appoint a group leader.

Correcting oral mistakes
When correcting students, be sensitive and realistic about what you can expect at their level. Give them an opportunity to correct their own or each others' mistakes whenever possible.

Focus on fluency rather than on accuracy when students are engaging in communicative activities such as pairwork and talking about themselves. You can note down any important and recurring errors and go over them with the whole class at the end of the lesson.

Try to focus on content as well as on accuracy, and respond accordingly if something is interesting.

Correcting written work
Make your corrections clear by indicating the type of error, for example, vocabulary, grammar, spelling etc. Comment positively on content where applicable, e.g. *This is very interesting, Carlos.*

Again, bear in mind the student's level and the focus of the activity, as you may not want to correct every mistake.

Enjoy it
We hope that the material in *Messages* 1 will motivate the students and facilitate their learning, and that the way the material has been structured will make your job as straightforward and effective as possible. Most of all, we hope it proves a rewarding experience for you and your students.

Module 1

Facts

See page 7 of the Introduction for ideas on how to use the Module opening pages.

Answers

1 b 2 c 3 d 4 a

1 What do you remember?

Unit 1 is a revision unit and has no specific Key grammar and Key vocabulary sections. The structures covered will all be dealt with systematically in later units. The aim of the unit is to activate some of the language which students have already learnt and which will be essential for communication in the classroom. It's important, wherever possible, to speak in English in your lessons and encourage the students to do the same.

STEP 1

Revision:

Simple sentences with *My name's ...*, *I'm ...*, *I like ...* and *I've got ...*

Some common words

Communicative tasks:

Making sentences

Giving personal information

- As an introductory exercise, revise greetings in English. Say *Hello* or *Hi* and encourage students to return the greeting. Then add *How are you?* and elicit appropriate responses: *Fine, thanks. / OK, thanks. / All right, thanks.*
- Ask students to turn to their neighbours and exchange greetings in English.
- When you come to the end of the lesson, say *Goodbye* and elicit the appropriate response: *Goodbye. See you tomorrow / on Monday / on Friday.*

1 Words

a
- Ask the class to say the letters of the alphabet in order from A to Z and write them up on one side of the board. Tell students to write the letters in their notebooks, leaving a space beside each one.
- Working as quickly as possible, students try to think of an English word beginning with each letter in the alphabet. Set a time limit of five minutes and get them working either individually or in pairs. Tell them not to worry too much about spelling and to move on quickly if they can't think of a word for any of the letters.
- Finding a word starting with *x* will be very difficult, so you may choose to leave out this letter or to supply a word yourself at the beginning (for example, *x-ray*, *xylophone*).
- At the end of five minutes, stop the activity. Go quickly

round the class to get several example words for each letter. If students had problems with more uncommon letters like *k*, *q* and *z*, you could give clues to elicit some of these words:

K: *king, key, kitten*

Q: *queen, quiz, question*

Z: *zoo, zip, zebra*

b
- Write the four lists on the board. Invite students to come to the front and add words to the lists. Alternatively, you could write up the words yourself as students suggest them, or appoint one or two confident students to do so. Check understanding by asking for translations in the students' own language.
- Remind students that it is a good idea to list new words in groups like this. The connections between them often make them easier to remember.

2 Sentences

a
- Look at the example and ask students to form another sentence starting with *I've got* (*I've got a camera, I've got twelve computers*). Then do the same with *I'm* (*I'm thirteen, I'm fine*) and *I + like* (*I like music, I like animals*).
- Remind students that we only use *a/an* with a singular noun (NOT *I've got a computers*).

b
- Choose two students to read out the examples.
- Give the class time to write at least two sentences about themselves. They can use the words in the balloons or they can add words of their own.
- Choose students to say their sentences to the class.

OPTION

With a small class, you could ask students to stand up and mingle, greeting each other and introducing themselves with their sentences.

3 Listening *Song*

a
- Look at the picture and ask students to say what they can see.
- Focus on the bottle and the jumbled words. Ask: *Can you make three words?* If students haven't seen these words before, there may be similar words in their own language that will help them to guess the English forms and to

work out the meanings. Ask them to identify the sea, the bottle and the message in the picture.

> **Answers**
> bottle, message, sea

b
- ⏹ Play the recording at least once to let students simply listen and enjoy the song.
- Give them a few moments to look at the jumbled sentences and to think about the correct order of the words.
- ⏹ Play the recording again. Students listen and read the sentences, concentrating on the correct order of the words when they hear them.
- ⏹ Ask students to write the sentences correctly. Then play the recording once again. Students listen and check.
- Check the answers with the class, but don't focus on punctuation at this stage.
- ⏹ Ask students to turn to the song words on page 144 of the Student's Book. Play the song again and encourage them to sing along. The second time round, you can divide the class into two, with one half asking and the other half answering the questions, and everyone singing the chorus together.

> **Answers**
> 1 What is it?
> 2 It's a message in a bottle in the sea.
> 3 It's in English.
> 4 Do you understand?

4 Punctuation

a
- Say the words in the box and ask students to repeat. If you think it is appropriate, ask them to explain the use of the different punctuation marks in their own language.
- Explain or elicit the meaning of *at the beginning, at the end* and *in the middle*.
- Students complete the explanation in the box. They can do this orally, in writing, or both.

> **Answers**
> capital letter
> full stop, question mark, exclamation mark
> comma

b
- Ask students to check their punctuation in 3b (the sentences from the song). Note that an exclamation mark could be used at the end of sentence 2 because the speaker seems to be expressing surprise and excitement.
- Emphasise the use of capital letters at the beginning of words for nationalities and languages (for example, *English*).

5 Writing *Information about me*
- This exercise can be done in class or set for homework.

> Ask students to write their sentences on a piece of paper and fold it. Collect the papers and put them together. Then ask students in turn to take one and read out the sentences, leaving out the person's name. The rest of the class have to guess who each person is.

> Revision:
>   Simple sentences with *I, he* and *she*
>   Classroom language
> Communicative tasks:
>   Communicating in the classroom
>   Reading a letter
>   Asking and answering about personal information

STEP 2

1 Classroom language

a
- Ask the question and brainstorm ideas, using the student's own language. As well as the suggestions in the box, answers might include:
  - *Ask a parent or an older brother/sister.*
  - *Ask an English-speaking friend.*
  - *Use pictures and examples in the Student's Book to help you.*
  - *Look at a grammar book.*

b
- Look at the example and ask for other things we can say in English. Write good suggestions on the board. Answers might include:
  - *I don't know this word.*
  - *Sorry, I don't/can't understand this.*
  - *Can/Could/Would you repeat that, please?*
  - *Can/Could/Would you speak slowly, please?*

c
- Tell students to check their list against the examples in the box and explain any new words (*guess, panic* etc.).
- Drill the expressions for things you can say, both in the box and on the board. Start with choral repetition and then ask individuals to repeat.

2 Reading *A message in a bottle*

a
- Make sure it's clear that this text is the message in the bottle from Step 1. Explain that some of the words are wet so we can't read them properly.
- Tell students to look only at the complete words, and to pick out any of these that they don't understand (for example, *Exeter, southwest, tortoise, Lightning*).
- In pairs, students ask each other about the words they have picked out. They may be able to explain or guess the meaning of some of their partner's words. If they

can't, they should use expressions from Exercise 1 to suggest a way to find out.

- Students follow their partner's advice until they are satisfied that they know the meanings of the new words. You will need to circulate so that they can ask you for meanings as necessary.

b • Still in their pairs, students try to work out the illegible words in the message. Tell them to look carefully at the surrounding words to help them.

- Look at the first sentence together before they start and elicit possible answers (girl or boy). Tell students that they won't be able to fill in the name of the writer at the end of the message, but they will find this out in Exercise 3.

- Go through the answers with the class, but don't confirm or correct them at this stage.

- Ask students about the writer of the message, without revealing that she is female: This person lives in ...? (Exeter.) Nationality? (British.) How old is this person? (Twelve.)

Answers
girl; England; twelve; music; computers; sister; a; called; nationality; What's; name
(Sadie)

3 Meet Joe, Sadie, Sam and Jack!

a • Give students a few moments to look at the photos of Sadie, Joe, Jack and Sam the dog. Introduce the names of the three characters and the dog and practise the pronunciation.

- Tell students to close their books. Introduce the recording (Listen to Joe, Sadie and Jack.) and ask the question (Who is the message from?).

- 🔊 Play the recording, several times if necessary. Students may at first come up with different answers – if so, discuss them together. (The writer isn't Jack because he lives at number 27, not 25. It isn't Joe because Sadie says her brother is 14, not 12. So it's Sadie – she's 12, and she's got a brother, a sister and a dog called Sam.)

Answer
Sadie

b • 🔊 Play the recording again. Students listen and read the paragraphs.

- Draw attention to the Remember! examples. Ask students to choose the correct pronouns and complete the sentences about Sadie. Teach or revise the word address.

- Students write out the sentences in full, supplying the correct information from the texts in Exercises 2 and 3.

Answers
The message is from Sadie because she is 12 years old. She has got a brother, a sister, a dog and a tortoise. Her address is 18 Maple Road, Exeter, EX11 4NP, UK.

c • 🔊 Play the recording of the message. Students listen and check their answers for 2b. Ask them what Sadie's surname is (Kelly) and write it on the board so that they can complete the message.

Tapescript
18 Maple Road, Exeter EX11 4NP, UK.

The 30th of August.

Hi! This is a letter from a girl in the UK. I'm English. I live in Exeter, in the southwest of England. I'm twelve. I like music and I'm interested in computers. I've got a brother and a sister. We've got a dog called Sam and a tortoise called Lightning.

What about you? What nationality are you? Where do you live? How old are you? What's your name?

Please write to me.

With best wishes from Sadie Kelly.

4 Writing and speaking More about me

- Elicit and drill the questions from the message in the bottle. Start with choral repetition by the whole class, and then ask individuals to repeat.

- Give students time to write their answers. If necessary, revise the names of students' nationalities.

- Choose students to ask and answer the questions across the class.

- In pairs, students ask and answer the questions.

Revision:	Communicative tasks:
Can I ...? for permission	Using numbers
Numbers and dates	Saying the date
The alphabet	Spelling words in
More classroom	English
language	Asking for permission
	and help

STEP 3

1 Numbers

a • You could start by using flash cards to revise the numbers 1–100. Hold up cards in random order and ask the class to say the numbers. (Alternatively, you could write the numbers on the board.)

- Look at the example. Ask the class to say the numbers (including the answer, 9). Then elicit the next two or three numbers in the series (11, 13, 15).

- Ask the class to say all the numbers in each of the other series. They then work out the next number in each series.

- 🔊 Play the recording. Students listen and check.
- Ask different students for their answers – they should read the whole series aloud. Then ask the class to say the next few numbers in each series.

Tapescript/Answers

1 1, 3, 5, 7, 9
2 2, 4, 6, 8, 10
3 11, 12, 13, 14
4 20, 30, 40
5 65, 70, 75, 80
6 21, 28, 35, 42

b
- Students now devise their own number series without letting anyone see what they have written.
- In pairs, they read out their numbers to their partner, who must write them down and try to work out the next number in the series.
- If there is time, students can form new pairs to repeat the exercise with different partners.

2 Dates

- You can again use flash cards or numbers written on the board to elicit ordinal numbers. Give special attention to the 'irregular' ordinals: *first, second, third, fifth.*
- Ask students to say the names of the months in order, from January to December.
- Ask: *What's the date today?* and elicit the correct answer. Drill the question and the answer, making sure that students say the words *the* and *of.*
- Read through the information in the Remember! box. Then ask a student to write today's date on the board. (It's good to establish the practice of asking for the date and inviting a student to write it on the board at the start of each lesson.)
- Ask the second question and elicit the correct answer in spoken and written form.

OPTION

Follow up with other questions, for example:
What's the date tomorrow?
What's the date on Saturday?
When's your birthday?

3 The alphabet

a
- Look at the photos and say the names of the characters, emphasising the vowel sounds in each one. Students repeat.
- Say the names again, followed by the letters with the same sound. Students repeat.

b
- Focus on the remaining letters in the list. Encourage students to say the letters aloud to help them decide which group they belong to.
- 🔊 Play the recording. Students listen and check.

Tapescript/Answers

KATE: Kate – A, H, K, J
LEE: Lee – B, C, E, P, T, V, D, G
MEL: Mel – F, L, M, X, Z, N, S
MIKE: Mike – I, Y
JOE: Joe – O
SUE: Sue – Q, W, U
MARK: Mark – R

OPTION

For further listening practice, give students a 'secret message'. Ask them to draw an empty grid of 7 x 4 squares. Read out the letters line by line, from left to right. Students fill in the letters, and then work out the message by reading down the columns.
(Answer: *Hi! My name is Sadie. I live in Exeter.*)

H	N	I	D	L	I	E
I	A	S	I	I	N	T
M	M	S	E	V	E	E
Y	E	A	I	E	X	R

4 Things in the classroom

a
- Ask students to look around and say as many words as they can for things in the classroom. Test their understanding by pointing to things and asking *What is it?* Elicit: *It's a … .*

b
- 🔊 Play the recording. Students listen and write down the letters. When they give their answers, ask them to say the word and spell it out.

Tapescript/Answers

1 R-U-L-E-R
2 D-E-S-K
3 W-I-N-D-O-W
4 D-I-C-T-I-O-N-A-R-Y

OPTIONS

1 Play 'Simon says', using the command *Point to …* and the words for classroom things. See Games, page 103 in the Teacher's Book.
2 Play 'I spy'. Write up the rhyme:
I spy with my little eye
something beginning with …
Say the rhyme and give the first letter of a classroom object. Students make suggestions until someone guesses the object you are thinking of. This person then starts the next round of the game.

5 Asking for permission

a
- Read out the three questions and ask students to match them with the pictures.
- Drill the questions, with students repeating all together and then individually. Pay attention to the intonation, with the words *Can I* being unstressed. For example: *Can I look at your dictionary, please?*

Answers
1 c 2 a 3 b

b
- Drill the two replies to the question.
- Give prompts to elicit questions and replies, for example: *Window? (Can I close the window?)* Shake your head *(No, sorry.)*

c
- Look at the example in 5c. Substitute some other words to elicit new questions, for example: *Door? (Can I close/open the door?) Pen? (Can I use your pen?) Book? (Can I look at your book?)*
- In pairs, students take it in turns to ask and answer.

6 Asking for help

a
- Make sure students can identify the people in the photo (Sadie and Jack). Ask: *Where are they? (At home / In their bedrooms.) Are they in the same house? (No – Jack is next door.) What are they doing? (Homework.)*

b
- Tell students to close their books and listen. Ask the question.
- 🔊 Play the recording. With books closed, students listen for the correct answer.

Answer   French.

c
- 🔊 Play the recording again. Students listen and read. They then put the questions in order and reply with true answers.
- Drill the questions *Can you help me?, How do you say ...?* and *How do you spell ...?* Give special attention to the pronunciation of *do you* /dʒʊ/, but don't discuss the grammar in any detail at this stage.
- In pairs, students ask and answer.

Answers
1 How do you say 'It's great' in your language?
2 How do you spell 'great'?

d
- Give pairs time to practise the dialogue. Encourage them to substitute their own names for *Sadie* and *Jack*. Students taking Jack's role can also substitute a question about English, using a word or phrase in their own language *(How do you say ... in English?)*.

- Invite one or two pairs to perform their dialogue for the class.

7 Writing   *A letter to Sadie*

- Tell students to re-read Sadie's message on page 8 before they write, and to make sure they answer her questions.
- Elicit some example sentences for the prompts in the example. Point out that the address and date go at the top of the letter.
- Walk round the class, giving help where necessary. Encourage students to ask questions in English when they need help.
- Collect the letters to mark, and choose two or three to read out in the next lesson.

Example answer
Dear Sadie,
I've got your message. My name's Pietro. I'm 12. I'm Italian and I live in Ancona. I've got a brother called Stefano and I've got a cat called Mimi. I like animals and I'm interested in films.
With best wishes from Pietro.

Extra exercises

The Extra exercises can be used flexibly, as consolidation, either during or at the end of the unit. The teaching notes explain how they can be exploited in class, but they can also be given as homework, depending on time available.

1
- Students write the questions in the correct order. Remind them to use a capital letter at the beginning.
- As you check the answers, ask for example replies to all questions except 3. For question 5, point to something in the classroom.

Answers
2 How do you spell your name?
3 What does it mean?
4 Can you help me?
5 What is it?
6 How are you?
7 Can I use your rubber?
8 Do you understand?

2
- Look at the example with the class. Ask students to suggest other replies that would be correct for this question (*Fine, thanks. / OK, thanks.*) Elicit questions that fit with replies b and c. (b: *What's your name?* c: *How is he?*)
- Students read the questions and choose the correct replies.

3
- Look at the example and the alternative answers. Ask: *What's Sadie's surname? (Kelly.) What's her nationality? (English.)*
- Students choose the correct words for the other sentences.

Answers
2 b   3 b   4 b   5 c

4
- Tell students that we use *and* (or *plus*) for the + sign and *is* (or *equals*) for the = sign. Teach *minus* (−) and *times* (x).
- Read out the example (*Fifty minus ten is forty.*).
- Students do the sums and give the answers in words. If some students finish early, they could work in pairs, setting each other new sums to work out.

Answers
2 thirty-seven   3 fifty   4 twenty-three
5 seventeen   6 fourteen   7 nineteen
8 ninety   9 sixty-four   10 eighty-eight

5
- Look at the example with the class. Ask: *Why is 'brother' different?* Establish that the other three words are names of animals.
- When you go through the answers, ask students to give reasons for their choices.

Answers
2 teacher   3 September   4 sea   5 university

6
- Test students' understanding of the sentences by asking them to suggest replies in English, for example:

  1 K-A-T-E.
  2 It means … .
  3 I can help you. It means …
  4 Yes, of course.
  5 Yes. What's the problem?
  6 Yes, of course. Here you are.

- Ask students to work on the translations in pairs or small groups, and then discuss with the whole class.

Extra reading

Alphabet world

Lead in

- Ask students: *How many letters are there in your alphabet?*
- Invite them to compare (in their own language if necessary) their alphabet with the English alphabet in other ways. Are there any consonants in English that aren't used, or are only rarely used, in their language?

Are there accents for vowels or consonants in their language that don't exist in English?
- If there are any differences in the forms of punctuation between the two languages, you could draw attention to these. For example, there may be different ways of indicating direct speech, or words that have a capital letter in English but a small letter in the students' language.

Task

- Introduce the words *vowel* and *consonant*, (and drill the pronunciation /vaʊəl/ and /ˈkɒnsənənt/). Say some English words and ask students to say if they begin with a vowel or a consonant.
- Explain the meaning of *symbol*. You could use Egyptian hieroglyphs as an example of a language that uses pictorial symbols.
- Ask students to read the text and match the letters from different alphabets with their names in the text. Check answers, then read out the text while they follow in their books.
- Look at the example (question 1) and ask: *Why is it false? (Because some alphabets use symbols, not letters.)*
- Students write *True* or *False* for the other four sentences. Ask them to correct the false sentences.

Answers
2 True.
3 True.
4 False. (It's from Cambodia/Asia.)
5 False. (It's got 6,500 symbols.)

About alphabets

For more on runes, see the background information for the first chapter of *The Silent Powers* on page 31 of the Teacher's Book.

OPTION

You can write out the runes with their English sounds, photocopy them and hand them out.

Runic alphabet

ᚠ	f	ᚷ	g	ᛄ	e	ᛗ	e
ᚢ	u	ᚹ	w,v	ᛈ	p	ᛘ	m
ᚦ	th	ᚻ	h	ᛉ	z	ᛚ	l
ᚪ	a	ᚾ	n	ᛋ	s	◇	ng
ᚱ	r	ᛁ	i	ᛏ	t	ᛟ	o
ᚲ	k	ᛃ	j,y	ᛒ	b	ᛞ	d

Use the above alphabet to write three or four simple English words, using runes. Ask the students to 'decode' the words back into English.

Are you ready?

Grammar:
  The verb *be*: affirmative
  Wh- questions
Vocabulary: Members of a band
Communicative tasks:
  Asking for and giving personal information
  Talking and writing about a pop group

1 Key vocabulary *Members of a band*

a
  ● Introduce the word *band* (using the photo) and ask students: *Who's your favourite band?*
  ● Focus on the photo and ask students to find Joe and Sadie. Tell them that the other members of the band are Lee, Mel and Barney.
  ● Read out the words in the list. Then ask: *Which number is the drummer / bass guitarist?*, etc. Students reply with the correct numbers from the photo.

Answers
2 drummer   3 bass guitarist
4 singer   5 lead guitarist

  ● Ask students to repeat the words.
  ● Point out that the word for a person doing a job or activity often ends in *-er* (*teacher, swimmer*) or *-ist* (*pianist, scientist*).

OPTION

You might choose to teach the names of the instruments here (*drums, guitar, keyboard*).

b
  ● Read out Joe's introductory paragraph, or choose a student to do so. Point out the example.
  ● 🔊 Play the recording. Students listen and complete the other sentences. Finally, students can write the complete sentences, if you wish.

Answers
(As for Exercise 1a.)

Tapescript

JOE: Hi! Do you remember me? I'm Joe Kelly. This is my band, Monsoon. Come and meet the others! Come and listen! I'm the keyboard player … And this is Sadie.

SADIE: Hi! I'm Sadie. I'm the drummer … This is Lee. Lee, say hello.

LEE: Hello, everyone. I'm Lee. I'm the bass guitarist …

JOE: Great. Thanks. And this is Mel. She's the singer.

MEL: Hi, everyone. Yes, my name's Mel. I'm the singer …

JOE: Brilliant! And this is Barney. Ready, Barney?

BARNEY: Yes. Hi! And my name's Barney. I'm the lead guitarist.

JOE: That's fine. OK. I think we're ready!

2 Presentation *It's called Monsoon*

a
  ● Choose students to read out the text. Elicit the meaning of *exciting, leader, brilliant* and *contact.*
  ● Students look at the three alternatives and choose the correct answer. Ask them to give reasons for their answer (in their own language if necessary).

Answer b

b
  ● 🔊 Play the recording while students follow the text in their books.
  ● Read out the questions. Students match them with the correct answers and write the answers.
  ● In pairs, students ask and answer and write the answers.

Answers 1 c 2 e 3 d 4 a 5 b

3 Key grammar be: *affirmative*

  ● Look at the example in the table. Point out that the apostrophe indicates the place where a letter is left out in the short form.
  ● To complete the table, students can find all the short forms in the text from Exercise 2. However, they may be familiar enough with these forms to copy and complete the table first and then use the text to check.
  ● Drill pronunciation of the short forms. Then ask questions about the characters for further practice: *Who's Mel? (She's the singer.) Who are Barney and Lee?* etc.

Answers
Singular: You're; He's; She's; It's
Plural: We're; You're; They're

4 Practice

- Students work individually to complete the sentences orally and/or in writing.

Answers

2 I'm   3 She's   4 They're   5 We're
6 You're   7 You're   8 It's

5 Key grammar Wh- *questions*

- To check students' understanding of the question words, elicit an answer for each of the example questions.
- Discuss the translation of the question words.

6 Practice

a
- Students work individually to complete the sentences in writing.

Answers

2 When   3 Where   4 Who   5 What

OPTION For further practice, you can write these questions and answers on the board. Students read the answers and work out the question words.

1 ....'s the date today?
It's 12th May.

2 ....'s your favourite singer?
Enrique Iglesias.

3 ....'s your school?
In North London.

4 ....'s your next maths lesson?
Tomorrow.

b
- In pairs, students take it in turns to ask and answer the questions. If they have done the option above, they can use those questions too.

Try this!
Answer: Yes! For example:
I is a very short word.
I is a pronoun. (*I like music.*)
I is the first letter of *ice cream.*

7 Reading and speaking *Band practice*

a
- Explain or elicit the meaning of *practice*.
- Ask students to read the email. Elicit the answer to the question.

Answer Joe

- Choose a student to read out the email. Draw attention to the greeting *Hi!* Point out that this is a very common greeting in emails.

b
- Draw attention to the use of *on* + day and *at* + time in the email.
- Students complete the dialogue orally and/or in writing. Call on pairs of students to practise the dialogue in open class.

c
- In pairs, students now substitute other activities in the questions and answer by using different times and places. Elicit some suggestions for answers about the place for the football practice, for example: *It's at the park / at the sports ground / in the playground / in the gym.*

8 Speaking and writing *My new band*

- To introduce the activity, you could announce your own band. The members could be a mixture of teachers on the school staff and music stars that students will know.
- Give students time to decide on their own band members.
- Revise questions with *Who ...?* (*Who's the singer?* etc.). Students ask about each other's bands. They can stand up and mingle to exchange information, or remain seated and turn to their neighbours on each side, in front and behind.
- You could ask some students to report back to the class on their partner's band.
- Writing the description can be completed in class or set for homework. For a model, refer students back to Mel's article on page 14. Encourage them to include some of the adjectives used in this article and in the dialogue with the members of Monsoon (*exciting, new, brilliant, great*).
- If there is time, they could design their own poster.

Example answer
I'm in an exciting new band. It's called Red Moon. Eva Fakos is the leader and she's the singer. Pete Stone is the lead guitarist and he's brilliant. I'm the bass guitarist. The other members of the band are Sandra Kotarska and Ben Jones. Sandra is the keyboard player and Ben is the drummer. Red Moon is a great band!

Grammar: The verb *be*: negative, questions and short answers
Vocabulary: Interests and activities
Communicative tasks: Asking and answering about interests

STEP 2

1 Presentation *Are they good at sport?*

a
- Look at the first photo and make sure that students identify Sadie and Jack. Ask: *Where are they?* (*At the bus stop.*) *What's Sadie got?* (*A letter, a photo.*)

Are you ready? **17**

- Look at the second photo and make it clear that this is the one that Sadie is holding. Discuss the two people. Ask: *Who are they? Where are they?* and invite suggestions. Elicit or introduce some of the key words, for example, *cousin, beach, Australia, surfing, swimming.*

b
- Teach the word *capital* by giving examples. Then ask the question about Australia. Invite students to answer, but don't confirm or correct their answers.
- 🔊 Play the recording. With books closed, students listen for the correct answer. (Note that Sydney is the oldest and largest city in Australia, but Canberra is the capital.)
- If you have a map of Australia, you could show the locations of Canberra and Sydney.

> **Answer** Canberra.

c
- 🔊 Play the recording again. Students listen and follow in their books.
- Look at the example. Ask why the answer is b: *Who is Sadie with?* (Jack.) *Who is her cousin?* (Annie.) *Where is Annie?* (In Sydney.) Point out that the question is asking about Sadie – so the short answer must use *she.*
- Students read the other two questions and write the correct answers. As you check them with the class, ask who the pronoun refers to in each case: *Who are 'they'?* (Jack and Sadie), *What's 'it'?* (Canberra.)
- Establish the meaning of *be good at.* Ask students to pick out other new words/phrases from the dialogue and encourage them to work out what they mean from the context.
- Drill the questions and short answers from the dialogue. Ask the whole class to repeat and then choose pairs of students to ask and answer across the class. Note that the verb should be unstressed in the question but stressed in the short answer.

> **Answers**
> 2 a   3 c

2 Key grammar
be: *negative; questions and short answers*

- Choose students to read out the first three examples. Elicit the full forms of the negative verbs (*am not, is not, are not*). Remind students that the apostrophe indicates the place where a letter is left out.
- Look at the example questions and short answers. Emphasise the inversion of subject and verb in the questions. Point out that in affirmative answers we don't use short forms (for example, we say *Yes, I am,* NOT ~~Yes I'm~~).
- Students complete the examples orally and/or in writing.

> **Answers**
> Yes;   No
> isn't
> are

3 Practice

a
- Students complete the questions with the correct verbs.

> **Answers**
> 2 Is   3 Is   4 Is   5 Are

b
- Ask pairs of students to ask and answer the questions.

> **OPTION**
> Ask other questions to practise short answers and to suggest some ideas for 3c.
> *Is Sadie from Exeter?*
> *Is Jack a member of Monsoon?*
> *Are Jack and Sadie cousins?*
> *Are you a student?*
> *Are [names of two students] in the classroom?*
> *Is [name of student] Australian?*

- 🔊 Pattern drill: TRP, page 11 (Unit 2, Step 2).

c
- Slower students can write one question, but quicker students can write more. They ask and answer in pairs.

4 Key vocabulary   *Interests and activities*

- Read out the words in the list.
- Ask students to match the words with the pictures. They will already be familiar with some words and others may be similar to words in their own language.
- 🔊 Play the recording. Students listen, check their answers and repeat the words. You may want to get students to repeat the word each time they check an answer, or you may prefer to check answers first, then play the recording again and repeat the words chorally. Point out the pronunciation of the *-ing* ending and the silent *c* in *science.*

Tapescript/Answers
1 computer games
2 cooking
3 reading
4 sport
5 art
6 swimming
7 science
8 music

5 Reading and listening   *A survey*

a
- Explain the meaning of *survey.*
- Ask the question. Students scan the survey quickly to find the answer.
- Point out the three choices for answers in the survey. Explain that *not bad* means *OK* – it's not negative but it's not very positive either. Similarly, *quite interested* is positive but not very positive.

b
- Explain that one of Jack's ticks is in the wrong box. Ask students to read the survey again and to guess which one it is.
- Introduce the listening. Make it clear that Mel is asking Jack the survey questions.
- 📻 Play the recording. Students listen and follow the answers in Jack's survey. Ask them to pick out the tick that is wrong and to say where it should go instead.
- 📻 Play the recording again. Pause to check comprehension of any new vocabulary.
- Drill the questions and answers. You may also want to drill some of the expressions in the dialogue (*Not really. Not bad, I suppose. What about ...? Great! Fine. Thanks very much.* etc.).

Tapescript

MEL: Jack, can I ask you some questions?

JACK: Oh, OK.

MEL: First question. Are you good at sport?

JACK: Sport! No, I'm not.

MEL: OK. What about art? Are you good at art?

JACK: Mmm, I don't know. Not bad, I suppose. Yes, I'm not bad at art.

MEL: Not bad. OK. And computer games? Are you good at computer games?

JACK: Yes, I am.

MEL: So that's yes. And what about swimming? Are you good at swimming?

JACK: Mmm ... not really. No, I'm not.

MEL: What about your interests? Are you interested in science?

JACK: Science? Yes, I am. I like science.

MEL: And cooking? Are you interested in cooking?

JACK: Cooking! Yes, I'm quite interested. I can make a brilliant spaghetti bolognese.

MEL: Great! So ... quite interested. Are you interested in reading?

JACK: It depends ... Yes, I'm quite interested in reading.

MEL: Fine. And the last question. Are you interested in music?

JACK: Er ... not really. No, I'm not!

MEL: So that's no. That's everything. Thanks very much, Jack.

JACK: That's OK.

c
- Students write true sentences about Jack. Choose students to read out their sentences.

6 Writing and speaking

a
- Students write at least three sentences, based on the survey – those who finish quickly can write more. Remind them of the prepositions: *good / bad / not bad at* and *interested in*.

b
- Choose two students to read out the example dialogue.
- In pairs, students ask and answer the survey questions.

7 Speaking *My interests*

- Read out the examples and encourage students to think of more questions to ask.
- In pairs, they ask and answer.
- Choose some students to report back on their partner's interests. Encourage them to use *and* or *but*, as in the example.

OPTION

As an alternative to Exercise 7, students could work in groups to conduct a class survey. They can choose questions from the survey in Exercise 5 but they should also add some of their own, for example:

Are you good at volleyball/maths/French/English/geography?

Are you interested in animals / pop stars / football/surfing/tennis/computers?

Groups join up with each of the other groups in turn to ask and answer the questions. At the end, you can ask them to report back on the results of their survey.

Vocabulary:	Communicative tasks:
Countries and cities	Talking about facts
Geography	Playing a quiz game

STEP 3

1 Key vocabulary *Countries and cities*

- Students cover the map or keep their books closed for this exercise. Ask: *What country are you from? What's the capital city?* If the English name for the city is different in form or pronunciation, encourage them to use the English version.
- Brainstorm with the class and collect names of other countries and their capitals on the board. Make sure that you include the following (as well as others that are particularly relevant to the students):

England – London *USA – Washington*
Canada – Ottawa *Australia – Canberra*
France – Paris *Italy – Rome*
Spain – Madrid *Greece – Athens*
Argentina – Buenos Aires

- Drill the pronunciation of the names.

2 Key pronunciation *Word stress*

a
- Ask students to read the words of Sadie's rhythm drill quickly first.
- 📻 Play the recording. Clap and stamp your foot to the rhythm of the drum beat and the words, emphasising the stressed syllables, and encourage students to do the same.
- 📻 Play the recording again. This time, chant the words of the places while you keep up the rhythm, and encourage the students to join in. Repeat this step if you like.
- 📻 Play the recording line by line. Students repeat, first all together and then individually. After each line, ask: *How many syllables?* and elicit the correct answer.
- You could ask students to practise the whole chant in groups of five or six, and then 'perform' it for the class. Alternatively, you could divide the class into six groups. They all say the first two lines together and then each group says one line of place names.
- Ask students what and where the places are, and help with any that they don't know (you can use the map).

b
- Look at the example and say: *England*. Show (by beating the stress with your hand) that there are two syllables and the stress is on the first one.
- 📻 Play the recording. Students listen and match the place names with the stress patterns.

Answers
America – 4;   Kilimanjaro – 5;   Spain – 1;   Africa – 3;

3 Writing and speaking

a
- Look at the examples. For the second sentence, ask: *Why do we use 'are'?* (Because *the Andes* is plural – they're mountains.) Draw attention to the use of *the* with mountains and rivers.
- Announce the time limit. Students use the map to write as many sentences as they can.

b
- Look at the examples. Give students a few moments to think about how they will turn their sentences into similar questions.
- In pairs or small groups, students ask and answer. If they don't know the answer to a question, they can use the map to find out.

4 Key vocabulary *Geography*

- Read out the list of singular words and ask students to repeat.
- In pairs, students ask and answer about the photos. For words they aren't sure of, you could teach these expressions: *I think it's … I think so too. / I don't think so. I think … .*
- 📻 Play the recording. Students listen and repeat.
- Draw attention to the plural forms, especially to the spelling of *volcanoes*, *cities* and *countries*. For notes on the spelling of plural words, refer students to page 142.

- Point out that we pronounce/hear the final *s* in the plural words.

Tapescript/Answers
1 mountain
2 river
3 country
4 volcano
5 lake
6 hill
7 city

5 Listening *A radio quiz*

a
- Introduce *quiz*. Ask students to give some examples of radio or TV quiz programmes. Ask for some opinions: *Is it interesting/exciting? Are the questions difficult?*
- Read out Lee's words. Tell students they are going to listen to the radio quiz called *Is that right?*. Explain or elicit the meaning of *right* and *wrong*.
- Students write down the words from Exercise 4 (singular and plural forms).
- 📻 Play the recording through twice. Students tick the words they hear.

Answers
city, mountain, countries, cities, lakes, rivers

Tapescript
DANNY: Good evening, ladies and gentlemen and welcome to *Is that right?* I'm Danny Green and our first contestant is Sally Walker. Hello, Sally.

SALLY: Hello, Danny.

DANNY: Are you ready to play *Is that right?*?

SALLY: Yes, Danny.

DANNY: Great! You've got three seconds to answer. So listen carefully, Sally. Is it right or wrong? Barcelona is in Spain. Barcelona is in Spain.

SALLY: Right.

DANNY: Yes. Madrid is the capital of Italy. Madrid is the capital of Italy.

SALLY: Wrong! It isn't the capital of Italy. It's the capital of Spain.

DANNY: Yes. Kilimanjaro isn't a city. Kilimanjaro isn't a city.

SALLY: Right! It isn't a city. It's a mountain.

DANNY: Yes. And you've got a thousand pounds! Well done, Sally! Do you want to continue?

SALLY: Yes please, Danny.

DANNY: Great! So listen carefully, Sally. Vancouver and Brasilia are countries. Vancouver and Brasilia are countries.

SALLY: Wrong! They aren't countries. They're cities.

DANNY: Yes. The Thames and the Mississippi aren't lakes. The Thames and the Mississippi aren't lakes.

SALLY: Right! They aren't lakes. They're rivers.

DANNY: Yes. And you've got two thousand pounds! Well done, Sally! Do you want to continue?

SALLY: Er ... Yes, yes please, Danny!

DANNY: Great! So listen carefully, Sally. The Great Lakes aren't in Europe. The Great Lakes aren't in Europe.

SALLY: Er ... Oh dear! I'm not sure ... er ... Wrong!

DANNY: Oh, Sally! I'm sorry. 'The Great Lakes aren't in Europe' is right! They're in Canada and the United States. I'm sorry, Sally. But never mind ... you've got two thousand pounds. Well done! And thank you for playing *Is that right?*.

b
- Choose students to read out the sentences.
- 🔊 Play the recording again. Students listen and decide if the sentences are right or wrong.
- As you check the answers, ask students to give correct information for each sentence.

> **Answers**
> 1 Wrong. (Madrid is the capital of Spain. Rome is the capital of Italy.)
> 2 Right. (It's a mountain.)
> 3 Wrong. (They're cities.)
> 4 Right. (They're rivers.)
> 5 Right. (They're in Canada and the USA.)

c
- 🔊 Play the recording once more, pausing after each expression in the list. Students repeat and guess the meanings from the context. Discuss translations together.

6 Speaking *A quiz*

- Students write their own list of right/wrong statements for the quiz.
- Invite different students to come to the front as contestants. Each contestant tries to answer questions from the rest of the class. They 'win', for example, £1,000 for each correct answer. You can add a bonus if they can correct the wrong statements.

OPTIONS

1 The quiz can be adapted for pairwork. Students take it in turns to be the presenter and the contestant.

2 Alternatively, you can set up teams. Each team works together to write eight right/wrong statements, and then they play against another team. When answering, they can confer briefly before they give the answer.

Extra exercises

1
- Look at the example with the class. Students then read the other questions and choose the correct replies.
- For question 3, ask students to say the question word that fits with answers a and c (*When*).

> **Answers** 2 a 3 b 4 c

2
- Students choose the correct words, a, b or c. If they aren't sure of any of the vocabulary, tell them to look back through the unit to check.

> **Answers**
> 2 b 3 c 4 a 5 b

3
- Remind students of the quiz in Step 3. Tell them that speaker A is Danny, the quiz presenter, and B is a contestant called John.
- Students choose the correct replies from John and write the letters a–e.

> **Answers**
> 2 d 3 a 4 e 5 b

4
- Students complete the missing words. If they can't think of a word, they should look back through the unit or consult the Vocabulary list in the module review (page 24).

> **Answers**
> 2 capital 3 volcano 4 band 5 football
> 6 leader 7 student

5
- Remind students of the question words – *Who* for people, *What* for things, *Where* for places and *When* for times.
- Look at the example and ask for a translation of *Christmas*.
- Tell students to look carefully at the answers when they are working out their questions. Note that there are various possible questions in some cases.

> **Example answers**
> 2 Where's Canberra/Sydney?
> 3 What's your address?
> 4 Who's Lee?
> 5 When's your/Joe's birthday? / When's the next band practice?

6
- Ask students to work on the translations in pairs or small groups, and then discuss with the whole class.

Are you ready?   **21**

Extra reading

The United Kingdom

All four countries in the UK are represented by Members of Parliament at Westminster (London) and they follow UK laws in areas like defence, foreign affairs and taxation. However, they also have their own national governments with power to create their own laws in many areas.

English is the first language of all four countries, but in Wales the Welsh language is commonly spoken and taught in schools. In Scotland and Northern Ireland the Gaelic language also survives, but it is less commonly spoken.

Lead in

- Drill the pronunciation of *the United Kingdom*. Tell students that this is normally shortened to *the UK*.
- Ask the question. Students should be able to name *England*, and they may know the names of the other countries in their own language.
- Students read the text quickly to find the answer to the question. Ask them to find the four countries on the map.

Answer
Four (England, Scotland, Wales and Northern Ireland).

Activity

- Read the text aloud. Teach or revise the compass points: *north, south, east* and *west*. Help with other vocabulary, for example, *don't worry, complicated, separate, prime minister, nearly everyone*.
- Write *England, United Kingdom* and *Great Britain* on the board and ask students to explain the difference between them.
- Focus on the map. Ask students to find the capital cities of the four countries in the UK (*London, Edinburgh, Cardiff, Belfast*) and practise the pronunciation.
- Ask students to say what they can see in each of the pictures around the map.
- Read out sentences 1–8 or choose students to do so. Elicit or explain the meaning of new words and pay attention to the pronunciation of Leicester /ˈlestə/.
- Students match the sentences with the pictures a–h. You can ask them to work on this individually or in pairs.
- As you check the answers with students, ask what they know about each place on the map. (This can be done in their own language if you prefer.)

Picture a: The Edinburgh Festival is a generic name for a group of festivals which are held in Edinburgh every summer, culminating in August in the International Festival (live arts), Edinburgh Military Tattoo (military bands), Fringe festival (the largest arts festival in the world) and international film and book festivals.

Picture b: Manchester United is one of the most successful football clubs in the UK. Its home ground is at Old Trafford in Manchester, where you can visit a museum of the club.

Picture c: Birmingham is a city with diverse ethnic communities. There are mosques and Muslim communities in most of the UK's cities and larger towns.

Picture d: The Channel Tunnel is the rail link under the English Channel, connecting Folkestone, in England, and Calais, in France. It was opened in 1994.

Picture e: The Notting Hill Carnival takes place every August in London. Notting Hill, a district of London, has a large West-Indian community and so the carnival has a strong Caribbean flavour.

Picture f: Newquay, in Cornwall, is known as the surfing capital of the UK, as it is said to have the best waves in the UK for surfing. It is a popular area for holidays, especially amongst those who like water sports.

Picture g: Leicester has one of the biggest Asian communities in the UK and is famous for its Indian restaurants.

Picture h: Lough Erne, in Northern Ireland, is in a beautiful area of rivers and lakes and is popular for fishing holidays.

Answers
2 h   3 b   4 g   5 a   6 c   7 d   8 f

Follow up with some further comprehension questions. For example:

Which country isn't in Britain? (Northern Ireland.)

Which country is in the north of Britain? (Scotland.)

Which country is in the southwest of Britain? (Wales.)

When's the festival in Edinburgh? (In August.)

What's the capital of Wales? (Cardiff.)

About the UK

BACKGROUND

Deliciously spicy curries started to become part of British cuisine in the days when India belonged to the British Empire. There are many Indian and Pakistani people who have settled in the UK, and it's normal for a town to have at least one Indian restaurant serving sit-down meals and take-aways.

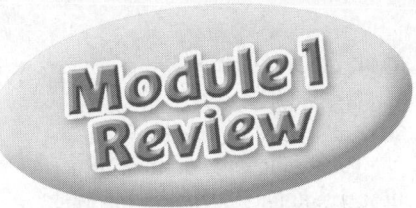

Module 1 Review

Language summary

1 The English alphabet

1.1 ● Students match the vowel sound in each colour word with the correct group of letters.

Answers

green – BDV;   grey – AHK;   blue – QU;
yell<u>ow</u> – O;   white – IY

1.2 ● Give students some words from the Vocabulary list to spell, for example, *surfing, guitarist, volcano, swimming.*

2 Numbers

2.1 ● Ask pairs of students to ask and answer the question across the class.

OPTION

Give each student a piece of paper with a number on it and set up a 'chain' question and answer activity. When they answer, they hold up their paper and give the number as their age.
A: *How old are you, Julio?*
B: *I'm 26! How old are you, Anna? (etc.)*

2.2 ● Ask the class to say the numbers in unison. Then go round the class, with students saying one number each.

3 Dates

3.1 ● Ask: *What's the date today?* Choose several students to answer the question.

3.2 ● In pairs, students ask and answer about their birthdays. They can ask several different partners. You could ask some students to report back on the information they receive.

OPTION

Photocopy a list of the students' names and hand it out. Students say their birthdays in turn (for example, *My birthday's on the seventh of June*) and everyone writes the dates beside the names. Use the completed list to ask questions, for example:
When's Marco's birthday?
Who's got a birthday on the seventh of June?
How many people have got a birthday in May?
When's the next birthday in our class?

4 Can I ..., please?

Answers

1   Can I use your ruler?
2   Can I close the window, please?
3   Can I look at your dictionary, please?

5 The verb *be*

5.1 ● You could ask students to write a mixture of affirmative and negative sentences.

Example answers

I'm Helena / I'm Spanish / I'm from Portugal.
I'm not English / from Africa.
Barcelona is exciting / a city / in Spain.
Barcelona isn't a country / in France.
Joe Kelly is 14 / British / the leader of Monsoon.
Joe Kelly isn't Australian / a guitarist.
The Andes are mountains / in South America.
The Andes aren't lakes / in Europe.
London is big / a city / the capital of England.
London isn't a river / in Scotland.

5.2 ● Choose students to read out the questions and others to answer them. Ask the class to think of more questions with *Is ...?* and *Are ...?* and elicit the correct answers.

Answers

Yes, I am / No, I'm not.
Yes, it is.

5.3 ● Students read the answers and write questions, using the table at the bottom of page 22.

Example answers

1   When is Christmas Day?
2   What is an anaconda?
3   Who are the Corrs?
4   Where is Timbuktu?

● Discuss the questions and answers with the class. Encourage them to guess the answers if they don't know them.

Answers

1   Who's Pavarotti? He's a singer.
2   What are the Alps? They're mountains.
    Where are the Alps? They're in Europe.
3   What's a BMW? It's a car.
4   When's New Year's Day? It's on 1st January.
5   Who are the Simpsons? They're a family in a TV programme.
6   What's Paris? It's a city.
    Where's Paris? It's in France.

6 Plural nouns

- Students say the plural forms. Ask for the spelling of *cities, countries* and *volcanoes*. Elicit example sentences using each word in the singular and the plural form.

> **Answers**
>
> mountains, lakes, cities, countries, students, volcanoes

7 Prepositions *in, on, at*

- Students fill in the prepositions.
- For the first sentence, remind them that *the twenty-fifth of December* is the way we say the date. In written dates we don't include *the* and *of*.

> **Answers**
>
> 7.1 *dates*: on
> 7.2 *days*: on
> 7.3 *times*: at
> 7.4 *places*:
> 1 in, in   2 in   3 at

8 Capital letters

> **Answers**
>
> Japanese, Monday, June, French, Washington, August, Italy, Thursday, Spanish, Argentina

9 Classroom language

- Check students' understanding by asking them to translate the expressions into their language.

Study skills 1 *Your coursebook*

- This exercise asks students to take a general look at the content of the Student's Book and the way it is structured, so they can use it efficiently on their own.
- Read through the questions. Refer students to the Map of the Book on pages 2–3 as a useful source for most of the answers.
- For question 3, point out the difference between the Vocabulary list for each module (organised by topics) and the alphabetical Wordlist at the back of the book.
- For question 4, draw particular attention to the Grammar notes section the the back of the Workbook.

> **Answers**
>
> 1 12.
> 2 6 (after Units 2, 4, 6, 8, 10 and 12).
> 3 Page 138.
> 4 In Key grammar exercises in the Student's Book units, and in the Grammar notes section at the back of the Workbook.
> 5 Page 25.

How's it going?

- Read out Sadie's advice. Explain or elicit the meaning of *Don't worry* and *No one's perfect*.

Your rating

- Students look back at the exercises in the Language summary and make their own assessment of how well they understand and remember the material.

Vocabulary

- The most suitable titles in the Vocabulary list for Module 1 are *Music, Subjects and interests* and *Geography*. Students test their memory of the words they have learnt in these categories.

Test a friend

- Other examples of questions about Module 1:
  Who's the singer in the band?
  Where's Exeter?
  Is Canberra the capital of Australia?
  Are Jack and Sadie Australian?

Write to your teacher

- This should be a regular feature at the end of every module. Use the students' letters to find out what they are enjoying and where they are having difficulties. Always reply to the letters with a personal message in the students' language, giving help, praise and encouragement.

Your Workbook

- Students should complete a Learning diary when they come to the end of each unit.

Coursework   All about me!

Facts about me

Students write about:
- their name and age
- their interests
- their address and telephone number
- their town
- their school

- Start by asking students to have a quick look at all six Coursework projects, pointing out that they will do one at the end of every two units. Explain that these projects will all link together to make a collection of material about the students' own lives and interests.
- The six Coursework projects can take any of these forms:
  - They can form a small book, with the pages stapled and a cover designed by the student.
  - They can be collected and kept in a special Coursework folder, with material added as students go on.
  - They can be made into posters and displayed in the classroom.
  - They can form the basis for a presentation to the class.

You may prefer to make a decision about the form the projects will take, or you could discuss it with the students and allow them to decide.

- Give students a few moments to look at Jack's project about himself in Module 1.
- Elicit all the information that students can remember about Jack from Units 1 and 2. You can prompt them with questions, for example:
  Who's Jack? (Sadie's friend.)
  Where's his house? (In Exeter / Next door to Sadie's house.)
  Is he good at sport? (No.) Maths? (Yes.)
  Is he interested in computers? (Yes.)
  Is he a member of Joe's band? (No.)
- Give students a few minutes to read the text. Check comprehension of any new vocabulary (for example, *with, near, skateboards, skate park*). Draw attention to the use of prepositions of place: *on the River Exe, near the sea, at Westover School, at the park*).
- Look at the artwork that Jack has used. Brainstorm with the students to collect ideas for ways of illustrating this project. For example:
  - a photo or drawing of a landmark in the town
  - part of a street map showing the street and position of the house
  - a photo or drawing of the student with his/her friends, family and pets
  - a photo or drawing of the student's home and/or school.
- Students set to work on their own *Facts about me* project. Set a time limit, allowing one or two weeks for work on the project. If students want to spend longer on this work, you could negotiate an extension of time. The work should mainly be done at home.
- Ask students to plan their text and check it before they copy it out and design their page. Tell them to use Jack's text as a model and remind them to look back at Units 1 and 2 if they need help with language.

Module 2

Things and people

See page 7 of the Introduction for ideas
on how to use the Module opening pages

Answers

1 a 2 e 3 d 4 b 5 c

3 What have you got?

STEP 1

Grammar: *have got + a/an; some/any*
Vocabulary: Names of everyday things
Communicative task: Talking about possessions

Answers

2 I haven't got a watch.
3 I haven't got any tissues.
4 I've got some crisps.
5 Have you got any tissues?

1 Key vocabulary *Everyday things*

- Focus on the pictures and ask students which words they know in English. Words like *pencil case* and *tennis racket* may be new, but they should recognise *pencil* and *tennis*. Other words may be similar to words in their own language.
- 🎧 Play the recording for students to listen and repeat. Pay special attention to the consonant clusters in *watch* /wɒtʃ/, *badges* /'baedʒs/ and *crisps* /krɪsps/.

2 Presentation *Have you got any peanuts?*

a
- Introduce the dialogue, making it clear who the speakers are.
- Read out the question and check students' understanding of *park* and *cinema*.
- 🎧 Play the recording. With books closed, students listen for the answer. Ask: *Who is saying 'Sssh'? Why?*
- 🎧 Ask students to tell you any words they heard from Exercise 1 (*watch, peanuts, crisps, tissues, umbrella*). Play the recording again. Students listen for the words.

Answer c

b
- 🎧 Play the recording again while students follow in their books. Pause to elicit or explain the meaning of new vocabulary. Make sure that students understand the meaning of *Have you got ...?* and *I've got.*
- You may also want to drill some of the expressions in the dialogue (for example, *What's the matter? Wait a minute. Never mind!*)
- Ask students to cover the conversation in their book. Look at the example and then elicit the correct answers for the other four sentences.
- Get students to repeat the sentences chorally, and then, once or twice, individually.

c
- Encourage students to act out the dialogue in pairs, pretending that the blackboard is the cinema screen and using appropriate actions.
- Ask one or two pairs to perform the role play. The rest of the class can take the parts of people saying *Sssh!*

3 Key grammar *have got + a/an or some*

- On the board, draw simple pictures of the nine objects in the table. (You can do this while pairs are practising the role play in 2c.)
- Focus on the verb form in the table. Elicit the full form of *'ve* (*have*).
- Choose students to read out each group of words in the right-hand column. After the second group, ask: *Why do we use 'an'? (Because the words begin with a vowel.)* After the third group, ask: *Why do we use 'some'? (Because the words are plural – they all end in 's'.)*
- Students complete the rules orally and/or in writing.
- Practise the example sentences. Say a pronoun (for example, *We*) and point to one of the pictures on the board (for example, an umbrella). Students say the full sentence (*We've got an umbrella*). Substitute different pronouns and different pictures.

Answers a, an, some

4 Practice

a
- Students work individually to choose the correct words.

Answers

2 a 3 some 4 an 5 a

b
- Give students a few minutes to write their own sentences.
- In pairs, they complete each other's sentences with the correct words.

26 Unit 3

5 Speaking

- If possible, start the activity yourself by talking about two things in your pocket and showing them to the class.
- Ask each of the questions and elicit some replies. Help students with any new vocabulary they need (*a purse, a handkerchief, a lunchbox* etc.). It's likely that they will want to include some uncountable nouns – in this case, teach the words with *some* (*some money, some chewing gum*) but don't focus on the grammar point at this stage. The use of *some* and *any* with uncountable nouns will be taught in Unit 7.

OPTION

Play a 'chain' game with *I've got + a/an/some*. Start with: *I've got an apple in my bag*. In turn, students repeat the sentence, adding a new item beginning with the next letter of the alphabet. For example:

A: *I've got an apple and a banana in my bag.*

B: *I've got an apple, a banana and some crisps in my bag.*

C: *I've got …*

Allow students to prompt each other so that no one gets stuck.

6 Key pronunciation *Plural nouns*

a
- Ask students to read the rhythm drill before they listen. Explain or elicit the meaning of any new words.
- Play the recording. Students listen and read.
- Play the recording again, say the lines aloud and encourage the students to join in. Beat time or click your fingers to emphasise the rhythm.
- Play the recording line by line and ask students to repeat. Pay attention to the stress on the nouns and the unstressed /ə/ in *some*. Also note the sound links before words starting with a vowel, for example:

cameras and CDs.

b
- Play the recording of the word groups. Students listen and repeat. Emphasise the extra syllable for the *-es* ending in *badges, cases* and *watches.*
- Use the chant to drill the words, first on their own and then in clusters, for example:

badges

some badges

I've got some badges

I've got some badges and some watches.

- Students say the whole chant together with the recording, then on their own.

7 Key grammar have got + some/any

- Read out the three example sentences with *some* and *any*.
- Draw attention to the negative and question forms of *have got*, and to the use of *any* in these sentences.
- Students complete the explanation orally and/or in writing. (Note that *some* can also be used in certain questions: *Can I have some potatoes? Would you like some bread?* However, don't introduce this complication here.)
- Return to the question and drill the short answers. You could substitute other pronouns (*we, they*) in the question to elicit *Yes, we/they have* and *No, we/they haven't.*

Answers some; any; any

8 Practice

a
- Students write sentences about themselves. When checking the answers, make sure they are using *some* and *any* correctly.

b
- Choose students to ask and answer across the class or set them working in pairs.

c
- Encourage students to think of more questions and ask and answer.
  Pattern drills: TRP, page 11 (Unit 3, Step 1).

9 Writing and speaking *My school shop*

- Teach or revise *shop* and *manager*.
- Read through the instruction carefully and check that students are clear about the difference between *useful* and *interesting*.
- Give students time to think about the things they want in their shop.
- Look at the example dialogue. Invite a few different suggestions for the second question, and elicit answers.
- Students ask and answer in pairs. Make sure they exchange roles so that each partner has a chance to be the manager.
- You could ask a few pairs to perform their dialogue for the class.

Grammar:
  Apostrophe: possessive *'s*
  Possessive adjectives
  this/these, that/those
Communicative tasks:
  Identifying things
  Talking about people's belongings

STEP 2

1 Presentation *That's Joe's lunchbox*

a
- Ask students to look at each photo and to say what they can see. Make sure they identify Sadie, Joe and their mother and father (Mr and Mrs Kelly).

b
- Read out the introduction to the dialogue. Explain or elicit the meaning of *kitchen* and *in a hurry*. Teach students the word *stairs*.
- 🔊 Play the recording. Students listen and follow in their books.
- 🔊 Play the recording again. Pause and ask students to identify the items by number in the photos. Tell them that *mobile* is short for *mobile phone*.
- Practise the pronunciation of the words in the photos.
- Students could practise reading the dialogue aloud in groups of four.

Answers
1 lunchbox   2 sandwiches   3 anorak   4 mobile
5 umbrella   6 football socks   7 trainers   8 watch

c
- Choose students to read out the eight sentences.
- 🔊 Play the recording again. Students read, then write in their notebooks if the sentences are true or false. As you check the answers, ask for corrections for the false sentences.

Answers
1 True.
2 False. (They're Joe's trainers.)
3 False. (They're Joe's football socks.)
4 False. (It's Sadie's umbrella.)
5 True.
6 True.
7 False. (It's Joe's mobile.)
8 True.

OPTION

Use the photos in Exercise 1 for the 'Picture memory game' – see Games, page 103 of the Teacher's Book. Teams take it in turns to say a true sentence about the photos (for example: *The sandwiches are on the table. Sadie's watch is on the stairs.*).

2 Key grammar *possessive 's*

- Discuss the translation with the students.
- Draw attention to the apostrophe in the examples. Point out that the apostrophe goes after the person who owns something (and that in this case it doesn't represent a missing letter).
- Make it clear that this possessive form is used with other nouns, not only with names. For example:
  My friend's mother is French.
  The cat's name is Thomas.

- You might choose to deal with plural examples here also. For example:
  This is my brothers' room. (= belonging to my brothers)

3 Practice

- Look at the example. Make it clear that the words in A and B need to be linked by *is* or *are*.
- Students work individually to match the items and write out the complete sentences. You could tell them to look back to the message from Sadie on page 8 if they can't remember some information.
- Allow students to compare and discuss answers with a partner before you check with the whole class.
- Point out that if two people are the owners of something, the *'s* comes at the end of the second name only (for example, *Joe and Sadie's dog*).

Answers
2   Joe is Kate's brother.
3   Sam is Joe and Sadie's dog.
4   Lightning is Sadie's tortoise.
5   Annie and Mark are Joe and Sadie's cousins.
6   Sadie is Lisa's best friend.

🔊 Pattern drill: page 11 TRP, (Unit 3, Step 2).

4 Key grammar *Possessive adjectives*

- Students complete the list with possessive adjectives.
- Draw attention to the difference between *his* and *her*.
- Point out that, like all adjectives in English, these words don't change their form, whether the noun described is singular or plural, masculine or feminine.

Answers
you – your;   he – his;   she – her;
we – our;   you – your

5 Practice

- Students complete the sentences orally and/or in writing.
- If students ask about the use of *hasn't* rather than *haven't* in question 2, explain briefly but don't spend a lot of time on this point. The use of *has/hasn't got* is taught in Unit 4.

Answers
2 his   3 their   4 his   5 her   6 your

6 Listening *Two famous sisters*

Venus Williams (born 1980) and her younger sister Serena (born 1981) grew up in a poor area of Los Angeles. Coached by their father, both girls started playing tennis at four years of age and turned professional at 14. At 17, Venus reached the final of the US Open, but it was Serena who first won the title in 1999, and in that year both sisters were ranked among the top five players in the world. In 2000 Venus won at Wimbledon, the US Open and the Sydney Olympics, while teaming up with Serena for doubles victories. In 2002 Serena beat Venus in the finals of the French, US and Australian Opens and Wimbledon. The sisters grew up as both competitive rivals and close friends, coached and managed by their father.

a ● Elicit information from the class about the Williams sisters. Establish their names (Venus and Serena) and their sport (tennis).

b ● Read the six questions and ask students to predict the answers.
 ● 📻 Play the recording. Students listen and match the questions with the answers.

Answers

2 f   3 e   4 a   5 d   6 b

Tapescript

The Williams sisters are famous tennis players. Their names are Venus and Serena. Venus Williams is on the left of the photo and her sister Serena is on the right. Their father's name is Richard and their mother's name is Oracene. Venus and Serena travel all over the world, but their favourite place is their house in Florida.

● Focus on the pronouns in the Remember! box. Remind students that *this* and *these* refer to things that are close to the speaker, while *that* and *those* refer to things at some distance away.

● You could point out that the words can also be used as adjectives, for example: *This watch is American. Those trainers are nice.*

Practise the pronouns with a 'chain' activity. In turn, students hold up or point to one or more objects in the room and ask about it. For example:

A: *Elena, what's this?*
B: *It's a ruler. Roberto, what are those?*
C: *They're windows. David, what's that?*
D: *It's ...*

7 Speaking *My things*

● Ask students in turn to bring one possession (or a collection of possessions) to the front of the class and put it on your table. Before putting it down, they hold it up for everyone to see and say what it is, for example: *This is my mobile. / These are my pencils.*

● Hold up one or more of the students' possessions and ask: *What's this?* or *What are these?* Elicit the correct answer with *It's* or *They're*, and give the object(s) back to their owner(s). Name a student to come to the front to ask the next question, and continue in the same way until all the objects are gone.

● Make sure that students say the /s/ for the possessive *'s* ending when they name the owner of any of the objects.

Vocabulary: Families

Communicative task: Writing a description of a family

1 Key vocabulary *Families*

a ● Focus on the pictures. Point out Lucy and explain that the other people are members of her family, gathered around her new-born baby brother. Ask them to find the baby's name (Robbie).

● Go through the words in the list. Refresh students' memory of the words they know and teach any that are new. You may decide to add *grandchild(ren), grandson* and *granddaughter* to the list.

● Practise the pronunciation. Give particular attention to *son* /sʌn/, *daughter* /ˈdɔːtə/, *aunt* /ɑːnt/ and *cousin* /ˈkʌzn/.

● Set a time limit of three minutes for students to complete the sentences. They could work in pairs.

● 📻 Play the recording. Students listen and check their answers and say the complete sentences.

Answers

2 grandfather   3 aunt   4 uncle   5 son
6 cousin   7 sister

Tapescript

VAL: Hello, dear! I'm Val. I'm your grandmother.

ERIC: Hello, Robbie. I'm your grandfather, Eric. Pleased to meet you.

LINDA: Hi, Robbie. I'm Linda. I'm your mum's sister. I'm your aunt.

BILL: I'm Bill, Linda's husband. I'm your uncle. And this is our son, Pete.

PETE: Hi! I'm your cousin.

LUCY: Hi, Robbie. It's nice to see you. I'm Lucy. I'm your sister.

b
- Focus on each person in turn in the picture and ask students to say their names.
- Students complete the sentences orally and/or in writing.

> **Answers**
> 2 Eric is Robbie's grandfather.
> 3 Linda is Robbie's aunt.
> 4 Bill is Robbie's uncle.
> 5 Pete is Robbie's cousin.
> 6 Lucy is Robbie's sister.

c
- It may help students with this if you get their help to draw a family tree on the board.

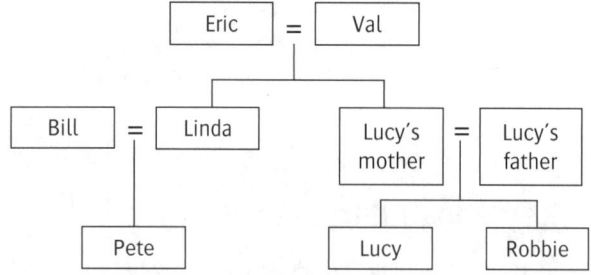

- Other examples of questions:
  Who is Robbie's father's daughter? (Lucy.)
  Who is Pete's father's wife's mother? (Val.)
  Who is Robbie's aunt's son's grandfather? (Eric.)
- Invite some students to read out their sentences and ask the rest of the class to work out the answers.

2 Reading *A new baby*

a
- Ask students to read the text quickly to find the answer to the question. Ask them to explain what type of text it is, in their own language. (It's an announcement that the parents have put in a newspaper to tell people about the birth of their son.)
- Explain the meaning of the new words in the text: *pleased*, *announce* and *birth*.

> **Answer** Cooper.

b
- Students use all the information they have about Lucy's family to complete the sentences. Check answers with the class.

> **Answers**
> 2 sisters, brother   3 Lucy, Robbie
> 4 Zahrah   5 son, daughter   6 Zahrah, Nick

3 Writing and speaking *My family*

- Allow students to choose which topic they will write about. Remind them of sentence openings they can use:
  I've got …
  His/Her name is …
  He's/She's/They're …
- To prepare for the first topic, read out the example and ask the students to work out who the person is (*Lisa Simpson in the TV series The Simpsons*). Invite them to suggest some more information they could add to the description of her family.

> **Example answer**
> I've got a brother and a baby sister. My brother's name is Bart and my sister's name is Maggie. My parents are Homer and Marge. I've got two aunts, Patty and Selma. We've got a dog and a cat.

> **Try this!**
> Answer: A is B's mother.

CHAPTER 1 The Silent Powers
Two messages for Sophie

BACKGROUND

The story *The Silent Powers* is based on a legend. The story is set in a place called Alderley Edge in Cheshire in the northwest of England. The Edge is a wooded cliff.

The legend says that under the cliff the ancient British king, King Arthur, lies asleep, surrounded by his knights and their milk-white horses. They are waiting for the day when England is in the greatest danger. On that day they will wake and ride out to save the country.

Many years ago a farmer was taking his beautiful white horse to the market. As he crossed Alderley Edge, an old man stopped him and asked to buy his horse. The farmer refused, but the old man said, 'Do as you please, but this evening you will sell the horse to me.'

At the market no one wanted to buy the fine horse and the farmer made his way home. As he walked across the Edge, the old man appeared again. 'Follow me,' he said. He touched a rock with his staff and a gate appeared. The man led the farmer and his horse into a large cave inside the gate. There the farmer saw the knights and their horses, all asleep, and there was a pile of gold and jewels. The old man told the farmer to take his payment for the horse. The farmer took some jewels and ran out of the cave in fear. When he stopped and looked round, the old man had gone and he could see only the cliff face.

The old man was Merlin the wizard, who lived in King Arthur's time, and he had chosen the farmer to provide a missing white horse for the knights. It seems that Sophie in our story is the next person to be chosen for this task.

Runes: The runic alphabet was a Germanic alphabet used in Scandinavia, Britain and other parts of northern Europe in early medieval times. When the Roman alphabet became the preferred script, runes fell into disuse, but their forms and meanings were preserved in inscriptions and manuscripts.

- Tell students that this is the first chapter of a story that will continue through the course. Explain that it is based on a real English legend. If you have a map, show the location of Alderley Edge, where the story is set. It's in the county of Cheshire, not far from Manchester.
- Focus on the picture and introduce Sophie. Ask: *What has she got in her hand?* (*A mobile phone.*) Use the picture to teach *cottage, horse* and *riding*.
- 📷 Play the recording (or read out the story if you prefer). Elicit or explain the meaning of *text message*.
- Ask a student to read out Seth's letter. Make sure that students understand the meaning of *lady*.
- Ask these comprehension questions and elicit answers from the class. Alternatively, you could write them on the board and ask students to write down the answers.

  1 *Where is Sophie from?* (*London.*)
  2 *What is on her mobile phone this morning?* (*A text message.*)
  3 *Who is the text message from?* (*We don't know – there isn't a name at the end.*)
  4 *Who is the letter from?* (*Sophie's brother Seth.*)
  5 *Where is Seth's new house?* (*Near Alderley.*)
  6 *What is Seth's house called?* (*White Lady Cottage.*)
  7 *Seth likes his new house. How do you know? Find a sentence in his letter.* (*'This place is fantastic!'*)
  8 *Sophie likes riding. Why is she pleased?* (*Because Seth has got a horse.*)

- 📷 To conclude, play the recording while students follow the story in their books.

Puzzle task

- Draw attention to the rune in the text message. Give students some background information about runes (see Background notes above).
- Introduce the form of the riddle. Explain that the seven letters – one in each line – make up the secret word, symbolised by the rune. (Note that the meaning of the text message itself will become clear later in the story.)
- Students work individually to discover the word in the riddle. Ask them to find out what the word means.

> **Answer**
> journey (Each letter of *journey* is in the first word but not the second word in each line.)

- Invite students to suggest reasons for the riddle. Why do they think the word *journey* might be important for Sophie? Allow them to discuss this in their own language.

Extra exercises

1
- Look at the example with the class and make sure that students can 'read' the family tree. If necessary, go through the names to establish whether they are male or female.

> **Answers**
> 2 wife 3 aunt 4 grandfather 5 husband
> 6 cousins 7 daughter 8 sister 9 children
> 10 grandmother

2
- Students choose the correct answer, a, b or c.

> **Answers**
> 2 b 3 a 4 c 5 b

3
- For question 3, make sure that students use 's with the last name only (NOT *Joe's and Sadie's sister*).

> **Answers**
> 2 Jack's 3 Joe and Sadie's 4 Lisa's 5 Serena's

4
- Go through the sentences and ask students to say whether the noun after the gap is singular or plural. For plural nouns, ask: *When do we use* some? (*In affirmative sentences.*) *When do we use* any? (*In negative sentences and questions.*)

> **Answers**
> 2 any 3 any 4 a 5 a
> 6 any 7 any 8 some

5
- Ask students to read the paragraph first. They then look at the alternatives and choose the correct answers.

> **Answers**
> 2 b 3 a 4 a 5 a 6 b 7 a 8 b

6
- Ask students to work on the translations in pairs or small groups, and then discuss with the whole class.

Extra reading

Collections

Lead in

- Explain the meaning of *collect* and *collection*. Ask about things that the students collect. How many items have they got? Where do they keep their collection? If you prefer, discuss these questions in the students' language, and ask if they know of any unusual collections that people have made.

Task

- Ask students to read the five paragraphs quickly to find out what each person collects. Elicit or explain the meaning of *model car, hair, chewing gum* and *packet*.
- Ask students to read again. Which collection do they think is the most interesting/valuable?
- Ask students to look at the example answers in the table. Elicit questions with the question words in the first column (for example, *Who is he/she? Where's the collection? What's in his/her collection?*)
- Students refer back to the text and copy and fill in the table. Point out that they should look for countries, not towns, for the *Where from* section.
- Ask some questions to test comprehension, for example:
  - *Who's got a collection of cars? (Subhail Mohammed Al Zarooni.)*
  - *What's in Steve's collection? (Chewing gum.)*
  - *Where are Fiorenzo's watches? (In a museum in Italy.)*
  - *Who's got something from Albert Einstein? (John Reznikoff.)*
  - *How many pens has Angelika got? (168,700.)*

Answers

2 Fiorenzo Barindelli, Italy, watches
3 Subhail Mohammed Al Zarooni, United Arab Emirates, model cars
4 John Reznikoff, USA, hair
5 Steve Fletcher, UK, chewing gum

---

4 Descriptions

Grammar:
Position of adjectives
What is/are ... like?
Vocabulary: Adjectives
Communicative tasks: Asking about and describing things

1 Presentation *My favourite things*

BACKGROUND

Dancing cans are novelty toys with parts that move when you wind them up.

The American film *Shrek*, an animated fairy tale released in 2001, is the story of a green ogre from a swamp, who sets out to rescue a princess.

Extreme sports are adventurous activities, often focused on individual performance, where people have to face dangers and take risks. Examples are skateboarding and snowboarding contests (where people perform dramatic stunts on their boards), kayaking and rafting in dangerous waters, barefoot waterskiing, bungee jumping and skydiving.

Sky surfing is similar to skydiving – participants jump out of an aircraft and do aerial stunts while in free fall, until finally opening their parachutes to land. In the case of sky surfing, their feet are attached to a board like a surfboard, which adds to the difficulty and gives more scope for acrobatic display.

- Ask students to look at the photos and say what they can see. Write key words on the board.
- 🔊 Play the recording while students listen and read. Pause after each paragraph and ask them to identify the speaker's 'favourite thing' in the pictures. Help with new words.
- Read out the list (1–5) and elicit or explain the meaning of the adjectives. Students match the items with the descriptions.

Answers
1 Joe 2 Mark 3 Lisa 4 Lee 5 Sadie

2 Key vocabulary *Adjectives*

a
- Make sure students know what adjectives are. Ask them to give some examples from their own language.
- Set a time limit of three minutes. Students find all the adjectives they can.
- To check understanding, elicit examples of things that

they think are easy, funny etc. Ask them to find three adjectives that mean 'very good' (*fantastic, brilliant, great*).

Answers
favourite, dancing, good, new, red, easy, fantastic, big, noisy, exciting, interesting, brilliant, happy, sad, funny, serious, extreme, great, dangerous

b
- Read out the lists and ask students to repeat. Make sure that they understand the new adjectives: *bad, boring, quiet, old* and *awful*.
- Students rewrite the lists in pairs of opposites. You could ask them to compare answers with a partner.
- 🔊 Play the recording so that students can listen and check their answers.

Tapescript/Answers

big – small	good – bad
happy – sad	difficult – easy
noisy – quiet	great – awful
funny – serious	exciting – boring
new – old	

c
- Students who finish early can use dictionaries to find other opposites (*long – short, dark – light, clean – dirty*).

3 Key grammar *Position of adjectives*

- Students read the examples and complete the explanation orally and/or in writing.

Answer before

4 Practice

- Students supply appropriate adjectives. Tell them that lots of different answers are possible here.

Example answers
2 big, noisy, exciting, great, small, old
3 noisy, new, difficult, exciting, easy, boring
4 big, new, interesting, exciting, funny, boring
5 new, exciting, good, great, bad, awful
6 happy, funny, great, serious, quiet, old

5 Speaking

a
- 🔊 Remind students of Lee's favourite thing from Exercise 1. Play the recording while they follow in their books.
- 🔊 Play the recording again. Pause after *What's it like?* and ask for a translation in the students' language. Drill *What's it like?* with the class.
- Students practise the dialogue in pairs.

b
- Choose pairs of students to read out the examples in the Remember! box. Elicit the full form of *What's* (*What is*) and emphasise the plural form of the question: *What are (they) like?* Explain that *like* in these questions is not a verb – it's different from the verb *like* in a sentence such as *I like dogs*.
- Point out that the answers to the question are descriptions, often using adjectives. The answer can give information about the thing/person (*It's got arms and legs*) or it can express an opinion (*She's great*).
- Choose two students to read out the example dialogue.
- In pairs, students make similar dialogues about the other characters, using the texts in Exercise 1.
- 🎙️ Pattern drill: TRP, page 11, (Unit 4, Step1).

Example answers
A: What's Sadie's favourite game?
B: *The Red Mountain.*
A: What's it like?
B: It's difficult, but the graphics and sound are fantastic.

A: What's Lisa's favourite video?
B: *Shrek.*
A: What's it like?
B: It's brilliant. It's happy and sad, funny and serious.

A: What's Joe's favourite TV programme?
B: *Extreme Sports.*
A: What's it like?
B: It's really great.

c
- Still in pairs, students ask and answer about their own favourite things.

OPTION

For extra practice, ask students to suggest examples of the following:
- a new building
- an old city
- a noisy street
- a sad song
- a boring TV programme
- a funny film
- an exciting film
- an awful TV commercial

Invite discussion. If there are disagreements, encourage students to express their opinions: *I don't think so. I think it's …*

6 Reading *Mark's 'Happiness recipe'*

a
- Introduce the words *happiness, recipe, ingredients, instructions* and *mix*. Explain that instead of telling us how to make some kind of food, the text is Mark's recipe for happiness.
- Students read the text and count the ingredients. Help them to guess any unfamiliar words (for example, *sunny, surfboard*).

Answer Seven ingredients;   No, they're not.

b
- Students read the recipe again and give ther opinions. Is it a good recipe for happiness? Are there things they would prefer to change?

7 Writing *My 'Happiness recipe'*

- This writing exercise can be done in class or set for homework. Encourage students to use adjectives from the unit in their list of ingredients.

OPTION

Ask students to design posters for their recipes, illustrated with their own drawings or pictures cut out of magazines. Display the posters in the classroom. You could have a class vote on the best happiness recipe.

Try this!
Answer: It's a table/desk.

STEP 2

Grammar: *has got*
Vocabulary: Adjectives describing appearance and personality
Communicative task: Talking about a person's appearance and personality

BACKGROUND

Robert Louis Stevenson (1850–94) was born in Edinburgh. Apart from *Dr Jekyll and Mr Hyde*, his most famous works are the novels *Treasure Island* and *Kidnapped*, but he also wrote essays, short stories and wonderful letters.

In English, the phrase *a Jekyll and Hyde* has come to refer to someone who is sometimes very nice and sometimes very nasty.

1 Presentation *He's got a cruel face*

- Ask students to look at the pictures and say what they can about them. Note the pronunciation of Jekyll /ˈdʒekl/.
- Read out the introduction to the text while students follow in their books. Elicit or explain new words: *scientist, potion, drink, change into* and *become*.
- Test comprehension by asking: *Who drinks the potion? Who is Mr Hyde?* Make sure students realise that Jekyll and Hyde are in fact the same person.
- Choose students to read out the sentences. Give examples to show the meaning of the new adjectives.
- 📻 Students complete the matching task, then listen to the recording and check.

> **Answers**
> Dr Jekyll: 2, 4, 6, 11, 12
> Mr Hyde: 1, 3, 5, 7, 8, 9, 10

Tapescript

The Strange Case of Dr Jekyll and Mr Hyde is a book by Robert Louis Stevenson (written in 1886). Dr Jekyll is a scientist. He has got a special potion and, when he drinks the potion, he changes into a different person. He becomes Mr Hyde.

Listen to the details about Dr Jekyll.
He's a nice person. He's tall. He's a kind, honest man. He's got curly hair. He's got short, fair hair.

Listen to the details about Mr Hyde.
He's got long, dark hair. He's got straight hair. He's got a cruel face and his teeth are black. He hasn't got glasses. He's got brown eyes. He hasn't got a friendly face. He's a dangerous man. Everyone is scared of him.

2 Key vocabulary
Appearance and personality

- a 📻 Play the recording for students to listen and repeat the words from the list.
- Ask students to list the adjectives under the four headings. Explain that some can be used in more than one list. Write the lists on the board.
- Point out the use of *tall* for people (as well as trees/ buildings etc.).
- Point out also that we use *fair* (not *light*) to describe light-coloured hair or skin.

> **Answers**
> *Hair:* long, dark, black, nice, short, straight, brown, curly, fair
> *Eyes:* dark, black, nice, brown
> *Height:* tall, short
> *Personality:* cruel, nice, dangerous, friendly, honest, kind

- b Elicit examples from the class and write them on the board in the following way:
  Mr Jekyll is ..., Mr Hyde has got ...
  Point out that with *hair* and *eyes* we need to use a form of *have got*. (Alternatively, we can say *His hair is long. / His eyes are brown.*)

> **Answers**
> Mr Jekyll is nice/friendly/honest/kind.
> My Hyde has got long/dark/straight hair. He's got brown eyes. He's got black teeth. He's got a cruel face.

3 Listening and speaking

- a 📻 Play the recording through once before the students start to write.
- 📻 Play each sentence and pause for students to write their answer. If they have trouble with any of the sentences, rewind and play it again or say it yourself.
- 📻 Play the recording through once again, pausing after each one to check their answers.

Tapescript

1 I've got straight hair.
2 I've got brown eyes.
3 I've got glasses.
4 I haven't got dark hair.
5 I'm quite friendly.
6 I'm tall.
7 I've got short, fair hair.
8 I haven't got curly hair.
9 I'm a dangerous person.
10 I'm not very honest.

- b Give students a little time to think of the things they want to say about themselves.
- Invite students to describe themselves to the class. Keep this brief and avoid anything potentially embarrassing for individuals.

4 Key grammar *has got*

- Look at the first two examples. Elicit the full form of *he's* (*he has*) and point out that *she* and *it* have the same form (*she's got, it's got*). Emphasise that the *'s* in this verb form is short for *has*, not *is* and point out the examples in the Remember! box.
- Focus on the question and elicit the short answers.

> **Answers** has; hasn't

5 Practice

a
- Ask students to try to guess the correct information from memory first. They then look back to photos in the Student's Book to check the information.

Answers

2 Jack hasn't got glasses.
3 Lisa has got dark hair.
4 Joe hasn't got curly hair.
5 Lee hasn't got blue eyes.
6 Sadie has got long hair.

b
- Choose two students to read out the example dialogue. Make it clear that student A should be able to work out which person student B is thinking of by asking just one question. The question can be about either appearance or personality.
- Ask students to suggest one or two other questions that A could ask (*Has he got fair hair? Is he tall? Is he a cruel person?*). Elicit the correct short answers.
- In pairs, students take it in turns to ask and answer.
  Pattern drill: TRP, page 12 (Unit 4, Step2).

6 Speaking

- Look at each picture in turn and ask students to describe the people. Elicit a range of answers with *He's/She's* and *He's got / She's got*.
- Invite different students to say a sentence. The rest of the class can guess which person is being described.

OPTION

As an alternative to Exercise 6, you could use the pictures for the 'Picture memory game' (see page 103 of the Teacher's Book). Give teams a few seconds to look at each picture before they close their books and start to make sentences about it. When they begin to run out of things to say, ask them to open their books and move on to the next picture.

7 Key pronunciation /h/

- Play the recording. Students listen and read.
- Explain the meaning of *hamster, heart* and *octopus*.
- Play the recording again. Students listen and repeat, following the intonation.
- Focus particularly on the /h/ sound, shown by the letters in bold type. Exaggerate the aspiration of this sound. Ask students to repeat the /h/ words on their own and then in longer clusters.
- Point out that some words are linked (by a line). Read them out so that students can hear the elision.

Play the recording once more for them to practise the links between words.
- Ask students to guess the answer to the second question.

Answer

An octopus has got three hearts.

8 Writing and speaking *Guess who!*

- Demonstrate by thinking of a famous person and describing him/her to the class. Students try to guess who it is.
- Ask students to choose their own famous person to write about, without naming him/her. The writing can be done in class or set for homework.
- Encourage students to plan their description by making notes under the topics in the Student's Book (nationality, job, personality, appearance). If they aren't sure of some facts, they may be able to find the information at home in fan magazines or on the Internet.
- In pairs, students take it in turns to read out their descriptions and guess their partner's famous person.

Example answer

He's an English football player. He isn't very tall. He's got fair hair and blue eyes. He's a great player and he's a nice person. (David Beckham)

Vocabulary: Parts of the body
Adjectives:
  Describing how you feel
  I've got a headache/cold.
Communicative tasks:
  Saying how you feel
  Describing an imaginary person

STEP 3

1 Key vocabulary *Your body*

- If students are uncertain about this vocabulary, you can revise by pointing to your own body, saying the words and asking the class to repeat.
- Set a time limit of three minutes. Students complete as many words as they can. They could do this individually or in pairs.
- Play the recording for students to check their answers.

Tapescript/Answers

1 head 2 face 3 nose 4 hair 5 eye 6 ear
7 mouth 8 hand 9 arm 10 leg 11 foot

1 You could introduce or revise some other body words here, for example: *stomach, tooth/teeth, neck, back, shoulder, elbow, finger, knee, ankle, toe.*

2 To practise the vocabulary, play the game 'Simon says' (see page 103 of the Teacher's Book). Use these commands:

Touch your face/foot (etc.).

Point to your nose/knee (etc.).

Open/Close your eyes.

2 Key vocabulary *How are you?*

- Introduce the question *How are you today?* and ask students to repeat.
- Focus on the pictures and read out the sentences. Students use the pictures to understand the sentences.
- Ask students to repeat the sentences. Pay particular attention to the pronunciation of *stomach* /ˈstʌmək/ and *ache* /eɪk/.
- Point out that *tired, fine* and *fed up* are adjectives, while *a cold, a headache* and *a stomach ache* are all nouns, used with *have got.* You could point out the difference between *I'm cold* and *I've got a cold* here.
- Choose pairs of students to ask *How are you today?* and to answer across the class.

3 Key pronunciation *Stress and intonation*

a
- Point to the stress patterns 1–6 in the exercise. Play the recording, which demonstrates the stress patterns, using nonsense syllables.
- Students match the sentences in Exercise 2 with the stress patterns in 3a.

b
- Play the recording for students to check their answers. Play it once more for students to repeat, imitating the stress.

Answers
2 a   3 c   4 f   5 e   6 d

c
- Students ask and answer in pairs.

4 Listening *Song*

a
- Play the song through twice. Allow students to listen to the melody and pick up the general feeling of the song.
- Introduce the expression *I've got the blues*, meaning 'I'm feeling sad'. You could tell students that the style of this type of music, originally developed by black American musicians, is also called *the blues.*

Answer Sad.

b
- Read out the adjectives. Explain *empty* and *heavy* and ask students to repeat them.
- Go through the sentences from the song and ask students to predict where the adjectives fit.
- Play the song again. Students listen and check their ideas. Ask: *Why is he sad? (Because his girlfriend is going away.)*
- Ask students to turn to the words on page 144 in their books. Play the song once again and encourage them to join in.

Answers
2 white   3 heavy   4 black   5 blue   6 empty

5 Writing *A 'SuperMe'!*

- Before students start to write, elicit a few more suggestions for 'super' parts of the body. Remind students that they can belong to anyone – male or female, alive or dead!

Example answer
I've got Michelangelo's hands. I've got Marilyn Monroe's legs. I've got Serena Williams' arms. I've got Mick Jagger's mouth. I've got Cleopatra's eyes … (etc.)

CHAPTER 2 The Silent Powers
Sophie's dream

- Ask some questions to revise the previous chapter of the story. For example:
  - *Who is the girl in the story? (Sophie.)*
  - *Who is she staying with? (Her brother Seth.)*
  - *What animal has Seth got? (A horse.)*
  - *Sophie's got a text message – who from? (We don't know.)*
- Tell students that in Chapter 2 Sophie is at her brother's house. Look at the picture and introduce the word *dream.* Ask students what they can say about Sophie's dream from the picture.
- Play the recording of the first part of the story (or read it aloud) while students listen and follow in their books. Help them to guess the meaning of new words by looking at the context and with the help of the picture.
- Introduce key words in the second part of the chapter: *garden, stone, lady, messenger.* Ask students to read the dialogue quickly on their own.
- Choose a student to read the part of Sophie while you take the part of Seth. Read the dialogue aloud.

- Ask these comprehension questions and elicit answers from the class. Alternatively, you could write them on the board.

  1 *Who is in Sophie's dream? (A woman and a dog.)*
  2 *What is the woman in the picture like? (She's got long fair hair and a white dress. She's kind and friendly.)*
  3 *What is the dog in the picture like? (It's a black dog with strange yellow eyes.)*
  4 *What is the woman on the wall of the cottage called? (The White Lady.)*
  5 *Where is Mr Neil's house? (It's near Seth's cottage.)*
  6 *Why can Mr Neil help Sophie? (Because he knows the story of the White Lady.)*
  7 *Who is the woman in her dream? What does Sophie think? (Sophie thinks the woman is the White Lady.)*
  8 *What about the dog in her dream? What does Sophie think? (She thinks the dog in her dream is Mr Neil's dog.)*

- 🔲 Play the recording once more, while students follow the story in their books.
- Ask students to practise the dialogue between Sophie and Seth in pairs. You could choose a pair to perform the dialogue for the class.

Puzzle tasks

- To work out the word represented by the new rune, students need to follow the instructions carefully.

> **Answer** message

- Students fill in the puzzle to find the dog's name. If they have problems remembering any of the words, tell them to look at the Vocabulary lists on pages 24 and 46.

> **Answers** CABAL
> (1 face 2 parents 3 numbers
> 4 mountain 5 curly)

- The rune suggests that Sophie's dream is a 'message'. Ask students what they think it could mean for the future. Who could the Lady be? What could she mean when she says: *'I am your guide – not here, but in another world'*? Discuss these questions in the students' language.

Extra exercises

1
- Tell students to think about the subject of each question to choose the correct word, *have* or *has*.
- If they aren't sure of the answers to some of the questions, ask them to look back through the unit to find the information.

> **Answers**
> 2 Has Lee got blue eyes?
>   No, he hasn't.
> 3 Have you got a stomach ache?
>   Yes, I have. / No, I haven't.
> 4 Have you got straight hair?
>   Yes, I have. / No, I haven't.
> 5 Has Sadie got a new computer game?
>   Yes, she has.
> 6 Have you got a favourite thing?
>   Yes, I have. / No, I haven't.
> 7 Has Jack got a friendly face?
>   Yes, he has.
> 8 Has Mr Hyde got a big nose?
>   Yes, he has.

2
- Elicit some example sentences using the alternative adjectives in questions 1, 2, 3 and 5.

> **Answers**
> 2 b 3 a 4 c 5 b 6 a

3
- For questions 1–3, elicit appropriate questions that fit with the alternative answers.

> **Answers**
> 2 c 3 b 4 a 5 b

4
> **Answers**
> 2 a 3 c 4 e 5 b

5
> **Answers**
> 2 a,c 3 a 4 b 5 c 6 a 7 a

6
- Ask students to work on the translations in pairs or small groups, and then discuss with the whole class.

Extra reading

London

London Zoo, in Regent's Park, was founded in 1828 as the world's first scientific zoo, for scientists to study exotic animals. It has been open to the public since 1847. Nowadays it runs conservation and breeding programmes for endangered animals.

The Science Museum opened in 1857 and now has more than 40 galleries of exhibits showing the major scientific advances over the past 300 years. It includes over 1,000 interactive exhibits.

The Imax Cinema has a highly sophisticated projection system and an enormous screen, 20 m high and 26 m wide. It produces a dramatic three-dimensional effect which makes the viewer feel part of the action.

Madame Tussauds is a waxwork museum which displays life-sized wax figures of historical figures and modern celebrities.

At 135 m high, the **London Eye** is the world's largest observation wheel. The passenger capsules can each take up to 25 people on a slow-moving ride which lasts for 30 minutes.

Lead in

- Before students open their books, ask them to say anything they know about the city of London (Big Ben, double-decker buses, black taxis, Tower Bridge etc.) They can offer their ideas in their own language, but you should write notes on the board in English.
- Ask students to read the text and see how many things in the list on the board appear in the text. Check comprehension of new or unfamiliar vocabulary (*sights, planets, amazing* etc.).
- Ask some questions to test comprehension, for example, *Where can you see a good view? What does IMAX mean? Where can you go if you're interested in science?*

Task

- In pairs or groups, students can make a list of sights, shops and museums in their capital city. These can be discussed with the whole class. For further practice they could write captions like those in the text, encouraging tourists to visit some of the places on their list.

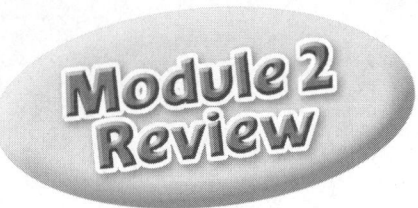

Module 2 Review

Language summary

1 have got

- Students complete the sentences with *have/has got* or *haven't/hasn't got*. If they can't remember information about the characters in the book, tell them to look back quickly at the texts in Modules 1 and 2 to find out.

> **Answers**
> 1 has got   2 [student's own answer]
> 3 hasn't got   4 have got   5 [student's own answer]
> 6 [student's own answer]   7 hasn't got   8 have got

- Give students a few moments to think about the question forms for sentences 1–8. Then choose students to ask and answer across the class.

2 a/an or some

- Organise a collection of objects on your table at the front. Cover them and ask students to write down all the things they remember. You could then ask them to make their own collection of objects on their desks and to test their partner in the same way.

3 some/any

> **Answers**
> any;   some;   any

4 Possessive adjectives

- Students work individually or in pairs to translate the sentences.

5 Possessive 's

- Students write about the relationships between the characters in the book. Remind them that when two people are named as the 'possessors', the *'s* goes at the end of the second name only.

> **Answers**
> 2   Sue Kelly is Joe and Sadie's mother.
> 3   Nick and Zahrah are Robbie's parents.
> 4   Robbie is Lucy's brother.
> 5   Kate is Sadie's sister.

6 this/that/these/those

> **Answers**
> [left to right]
> this
> these
> Those;   that

7 Adjectives

> **Answers**
> 1   London is a very big city.
> 2   He's got curly hair.
> 3   Mr Hyde is a dangerous man.
> 4   I've got a new watch.

> **OPTION**
> For revision of opposite adjectives, you can play 'Bingo' (see Games, page 103 of the Teacher's Book). Students fill their grid with nine adjectives from the list in Exercise 2a on page 38. As you call out the adjectives, they cross out the opposite adjectives in their grid.

8 Describing appearance *What's he like?*

- Students look at the painting You can tell them that the picture is called *Woman in blue tones*, by Paul Klee (or leave it to the students to decide if they think it is a man or a woman) and write a description of the person in the picture.

> **Example answer**
> She's got a blue, green and brown face.
> She's got black eyes. She hasn't got hair.
> She hasn't got ears. She's got a black mouth.

Study skills 2   Using a dictionary

1
- Ask students to raise their hands if they have got an English dictionary. Ask how often they use it. Is it difficult to use?
- Introduce a few other simple dictionary abbreviations for parts of speech and see if the class can work out what they mean. For example:
  v = verb
  adj = adjective
  pron = pronoun
- Students sort the letters and words into alphabetical order.

2
- Look at the three different uses of *can*. Ask about the meanings of *mouse*.
- Point out that a dictionary separates the different meanings of a word and gives examples. This helps us to recognise which meaning is the one we want.

Answer

A *mouse* can be an animal (*I've got a pet mouse*) or it can be a part of a computer (*Use the mouse to move to different places on your computer screen.*)

3
- Point out that English pronunciation of a word is often very different from its spelling. Explain that the phonetic symbols used in dictionaries can help with this problem.
- Elicit the correct pronunciation of the words. You could write them on the board as phonetic symbols, as an introduction to this 'alphabet' of sounds.

How's it going?

Your rating

- Students look back at the exercises in the Language summary and make their own assessment of how well they understand and remember the different language points.

Vocabulary

- The most suitable titles in the Vocabulary list for Module 1 are *Members of a family*, *Parts of the body* and *Adjectives*. Students test their memory of the words they have learnt in these categories.

Test a friend

- Ask students to think of other words and people to substitute in these questions. They then ask and answer in pairs.

Write to your teacher

- Use the students' letters to find out what they are enjoying and where they are having difficulties. Reply to the letters with a personal message in the students' language, giving help, praise and encouragement.

Your Workbook

- Students should complete the Learning diary when they come to the end of each unit.

Coursework   All about me!

Important things to me

Students write about their favourite things, places and people

- Give students a few minutes to look at Jack's project about himself.
- Explain or elicit the meaning of key words: *zip, present, film star, badger*.
- Ask a few comprehension questions, for example: *What's Jack's favourite film star? What's this animal?* (pointing at badger) *Who's Ben? What's he like?* etc.
- Write up the following headings on the board:
  Favourite people
  Favourite possessions
  Favourite places
  Favourite books
  Favourite films
  Favourite animals
  Elicit a few ideas for each one.
- Ask students to copy out the headings and quickly jot down some ideas of their own for each one. They should include some brief descriptive notes.
- Students select the things they want to write about from their notes and set to work on their own project at home. They should write at least four paragraphs and illustrate them as they wish.
- Set a time limit, allowing one or two weeks for work on the project. If students want to spend longer on this work, you could negotiate an extension of time. The work should be mainly done at home.
- Ask students to check their text before they copy it out and design their page. Tell them to use Jack's text as a model and remind them to look back at Units 3 and 4 if they need help with language.

5 My world

STEP 1

Grammar: Present simple: affirmative and negative
Communicative tasks:
   Talking about things you do
   Writing about teenagers' habits

1 Key vocabulary *Things you do*

a
- 📷 Focus on the pictures. Play the recording for students to listen and repeat. Make sure they say the /z/ sound in the verb *use*.
- To test comprehension, you can mime the actions and ask students to say the phrases.
- Choose someone to read out the example. Then ask students to make similar sentences about themselves.

b
- Help students to substitute other nouns that they can use with these verbs, for example: *read books, watch films, play football / the guitar, wear jeans, use a calculator, eat a lot of peanuts, drink water, go to a sports club / to the cinema.*
- Point out the difference between *play volleyball* (= game/sport) and *play the piano* (= musical instrument).

BACKGROUND

Vegetarians: Students may be interested to know that just under 25% of the world's population eat mainly vegetarian food, and there are about three million vegetarians in Britain. Leonardo da Vinci was a vegetarian, and so was Albert Einstein. Famous vegetarians today include Paul McCartney, Richard Gere, Kim Basinger, Madonna, Paul Weller and Michael Jackson.

2 Presentation *I go to a judo club*

a
- Before students read the text, you could ask them to tell you what they know already about Sadie and Joe.
- 📷 Read the question and explain *addict*. Play the recording while students listen and read.
- Elicit the answer to the question. Ask students to find the sentence which tells us that Joe isn't a computer addict. (*Joe doesn't use the computer every day.*)
- Choose students to read the text aloud. Pause at the end of each paragraph to help with vocabulary and practise

pronunciation. Point out that the verb with judo is *do*, not *play*: *Sadie does judo* (NOT *plays judo*).

Answer Sadie.

- Drill some of the present simple phrases from the text, for example: *I play hockey. I don't watch sport. Joe plays football. He doesn't like vegetables.*

b
- Look at the pictures and ask: *What is it?* or *What are they?* to elicit *basketball, computer, judo* etc.
- Students refer back to the text to identify the person for each picture. Ask them to write sentences as in the example. Draw attention to the *-s* verb ending.

Answers

2 It's Sadie. She writes a lot of emails and she uses the Internet.
3 It's Sadie. She goes to a judo club / does judo.
4 It's Sadie. She's a vegetarian / doesn't eat meat.
5 It's Joe. He reads horror stories.
6 It's Joe. He's got a bike.

c
- You could ask students to complete the sentences (in writing) without looking at the text. They then scan the text quickly to check their answers.

Answers

1 Sadie   2 Joe and Sadie   3 Sadie   4 Sadie
5 Sadie   6 Joe and Sadie   7 Joe   8 Joe and Sadie

3 Key grammar

Present simple: affirmative and negative

- Students complete the table orally and/or in writing. Emphasise the *-s* ending for the third person singular verb form. Elicit the full form of *don't* (*do not*) and *doesn't* (*does not*) and point out that both negative forms are followed by the infinitive of the verb (NOT *doesn't plays*).
- Make it clear that the present simple is not used for actions happening at this moment, but for things that happen normally or regularly.

Answers

plays
play

4 Practice

a ● Students supply the correct form of the verb *like* to complete the sentences.

🔊 Pattern drill: TRP, page 12 (Unit 5, Step 1).

Answers
2 I like / don't like vegetables.
3 Joe plays basketball.
4 I like / don't like sport.
5 Sadie doesn't like steak.
6 Joe and Sadie like music.

b ● Look at the example. Encourage students to write a few different sentences, some true and some false.

● In pairs, students listen to each other and decide if the sentences are true or false.

● You can ask several students to say a sentence and invite responses from the class.

5 Key pronunciation *Verbs + /s/, /z/, /ɪz/*

● 🔊 Play the recording. Students listen and repeat. Point out that the sound differences are the same as for plural nouns (see Unit 3, Step 1, Exercise 6).

OPTION

You could ask students to put the following verbs in the correct lists:

prefers, listens, loves, chooses, finishes, helps, guesses, speaks.

6 Writing and speaking

a ● Give students time to write three or more sentences. Encourage them to use *and* or *but* for related or contrasting statements.

b ● In pairs, students read out their sentences.

● Invite several students to report back to the class on the similarities/differences between them and their partner.

7 Reading *British teenagers*

BACKGROUND

Surveys suggest that British teenagers spend up to five hours a day **watching TV**.

The majority of schools in Britain have a compulsory **uniform**. It usually consists of a dress or skirt (for girls) or trousers (for boys and girls), with a matching jumper or sweatshirt, a jacket and perhaps a tie.

Radio 1 is a BBC radio station which mainly plays pop music.

People in the UK are very fond of **crisps** and other junk food. They are also the top consumers of chocolates and sweets in Europe. Some reports estimate that due to poor diet and lack of exercise, more than a million British children under the age of 16 are obese.

The British fall far behind other Europeans in their knowledge of **foreign languages**. The UK is the only EU country where language teaching in primary schools is not compulsory, and a survey in 2001 revealed that 66% of the population have no real knowledge of any foreign language.

a ● Ask students to read the list of characteristics. Check comprehension of any new words. Note that this is a profile of 'average' behaviour – it certainly isn't true of every British teenager.

● Discuss the information with the class and invite students to make comparisons with their own habits.

b ● Students use the list to write sentences about themselves. Ask a few students to read out their sentences.

8 Writing and speaking
Teenagers in my country

● This writing exercise can be done in class or set for homework. Encourage students to list as many points as they can. Remind them to use the *-s* ending for the present simple affirmative verbs.

● You could choose some students to read out their work. Invite the class to comment and discuss.

Grammar: Present simple: questions and short answers
Vocabulary: Scary things
Communicative task: Talking about fears, likes and dislikes

STEP 2

1 Presentation *Do you like heights?*

BACKGROUND

The seaside resort town of **Blackpool** is in Lancashire, near Liverpool. It is popular for its cheap and cheerful amusement facilities along 11 km of promenades, lit up by coloured lights known as 'the illuminations'. It has the world's largest roller coaster, 75 metres high and 1.5 km long.

The **Blackpool Tower** is a steel structure built in the 1890s. A lift takes visitors to the top of the tower, where the Walk of Faith was installed in 1994, and the building that forms its base houses an aquarium, an adventure playground, a circus and a ballroom.

a
- Ask students to look at the photos and to say what they can about them. Introduce the word *tower* and establish what we mean by *to be scared of heights*.
- Tell the class that the tower in the photo is in Blackpool. If you have a map of England, you can point out the town's location.
- Read out the paragraph about Blackpool Tower or ask a student to do so.
- Explain the meaning of *faith*. Ask students to suggest why this amusement is called the 'Walk of Faith'.
- 📻 Read the instruction and the question. Play the recording of the dialogue. Students listen for the answer.
- 📻 Play the recording again. Pause after the third and fourth lines and ask students to guess the meaning of *scared* and *terrified*.

Answer
No, she isn't. She's terrified.

Tapescript
REPORTER: Blackpool is a holiday town in the north of England. Every year a million tourists visit Blackpool Tower. It's got a glass floor 117 metres above the ground. It's called the 'Walk of Faith'.

Er … Excuse me! Can I ask you some questions?

GIRL: Er … yes …

REPORTER: Are you scared?

GIRL: Yes, I am. I'm terrified!

REPORTER: Do you want to walk across?

GIRL: Yes, I do. But I'm too scared!

REPORTER: Do you like heights?

GIRL: No, I don't.

b
- Give students a few moments to read the two lists. Ask them to think about how the questions and answers match.
- 📻 Play the dialogue again. Students listen for the questions and check their ideas.
- Draw attention to the use of *does* in the questions and short answers with *want* and *like*. Drill the questions and answers.

Answers
1 c 2 a 3 b

c
- Draw attention to the use of *do* and *don't* in these questions and answers, where the subject is *you* or *I*.
- Students choose their own answers to the questions. Make sure they recognise the difference between *quite scared* and *terrified*.
- Drill the questions and answers. Pay attention to the unstressed schwa sound of *Do* in the question. Contrast this with the stressed *do* in the answer.

- Ask for a show of hands to find out how many students in the class share a fear of heights. You can reassure them by telling them that this is a very common human fear.

2 Key grammar
Present simple: questions and short answers

- Look at the example questions. Substitute *I*, *we* and *they* for *you* in the question, to make it clear that we use *do* (not *does*) with all these subjects.
- Elicit the short answers for all forms of the question.
- Draw a contrast with questions and answers using the verb *be*. Remind students that we do not use any form of *do* with the verb *be*.

Answers
does
don't
Explanation: does

3 Practice

a
- Choose one or two students to say each question. Then ask the class to repeat.

b
- In pairs, students take it in turns to ask and answer. If they aren't sure about any of the information about Joe and Sadie, they can look back quickly to the text on page 50.

Answers
1 Does Sadie like tomato ketchup? Yes, she does.
2 Does Sadie watch sport on TV? No, she doesn't.
3 Does Sadie eat meat? No, she doesn't.
4 Does Joe like vegetables? No, he doesn't.
5 Does Joe read horror stories? Yes, he does.

4 Speaking

a
- Ask students to give a few examples of horror films, funny films, comics etc.
- In pairs, students ask and answer.

b
- Encourage students who finish quickly to add new questions. They could use the verbs in the box or they could choose others. For example: *Do you eat / wear / go to …?*

For further practice, you can play 'Find someone who ...'. Students copy down a list of activities, for example:

Find someone who ...

lives near the school.	*doesn't like fish.*
reads a lot of books.	*plays the piano.*
doesn't eat meat.	*plays basketball.*
wears black trainers.	*walks to school.*

Students mingle and ask questions (*Do you live near the school?* etc.) until they can find a name for each activity.

5 Key vocabulary *Scary things*

According to a survey, people's most common fears are: 1 spiders, 2 people / social situations, 3 flying, 4 open spaces, 5 confined spaces, 6 heights, 7 vomiting, 8 cancer, 9 thunderstorms.

Some of the strangest include fear of beards, chickens, dolls, string and the colour purple!

● Look at the person in the picture. Ask *What's the matter?* to elicit the answer *She's scared/terrified.*

● Read out the words in the list.

● Set a time limit of two minutes and ask students to try to match the words with the numbered items in the picture. They could work on this in pairs. You could tell them that UFO stands for *unidentified flying object* and translate this phrase literally for them.

● 🎙 Play the recording for students to check their answers and repeat the words.

● To test comprehension, give definitions and ask students to say the words. For example:

An animal with eight legs. (spider)

An animal that goes out at night. (bat)

An animal in the sea. (shark)

A noisy sound in the sky. (thunder)

Someone from another world. (alien)

● Ask students which of these things they are scared of. You could start off by describing a fear of your own, to help them feel relaxed about talking on this subject.

Tapescript/Answers

1	the dark	6	rat
2	thunder	7	spider
3	UFO	8	vampire
4	alien	9	bat
5	shark	10	ghost

6 Listening *Song*

a ● 🎙 Read out the titles and then play the song. Students choose the best title.

Answer Scared.

b ● 🎙 Play the song again. Help the students with new vocabulary, for example, *tremble, believe in, hide, pillow.*

● 🎙 Students complete the sentences in writing. They then listen again to check their answers.

Answers

1 Are   2 Do   3 scared   4 believe

c ● Students form more questions with words from Exercise 5. Choose students to ask and answer across the class.

● 🎙 Ask students to turn to the song words on page 144. Play the song once again for them to join in.

🎙 Pattern drills: TRP, see page 12 (Unit 5, Step2).

7 Writing and speaking *A questionnaire*

● Look at the example. Ask students to write similar questions on two of the listed topics.

● Students use their questionnaire to interview other students.

Example questions

Films: Do you watch films on TV? Do you go to the cinema? What's your favourite film? Who's your favourite film star?

Try this!

Answer: A tarantula.

(Also known as the wolf spider, the tarantula is a large hairy hunting spider, with a body about 2.5 cm long.)

Grammar:

   Question forms (revision)

   Wh- questions

Communicative task: Writing a conversation about everyday life

1 Presentation *Where do you come from?*

● Focus on the strange figure in the picture and ask *Who is he? What's he like?* Establish that he's an alien from outer space, and the child is asking him questions.

● Read out the questions or choose students to do so. Explain the question *What sort of ...?*. Ask them to repeat the questions.

- Give students time to read the answers. Help with new vocabulary (*planet, meet, Queen*).
- Students complete the matching task. They could do this individually or in pairs.
- 🔊 Play the recording. Students listen and check their answers.
- Point out that in Exercise 1, questions 1, 3, 6 and 7 lead to a *Yes* or *No* answer, However, those starting with question words need an answer that gives some kind of information.
- Remind students that questions with the verb *be* are formed simply by inverting the subject and verb. For other present simple verbs, we have to use *do* or *does*.
- Ask students to practise the questions and answers in pairs.
- Ask students to suggest some other possible answers for questions 2–8.

Answers

1 h 2 e 3 f 4 b 5 g 6 c 7 a 8 d

2 Key grammar Wh- *questions*

- Ask students to translate the question words into their own language. They then complete the table orally and/or in writing.
- Choose students to read out the questions, using the subject *he*, and elicit possible answers about the alien.
- You could add another question using *When ...?*, for example: *When does he eat his lunch?*
- Remind students that these present simple questions and answers are about things that happen normally or regularly.

Answers

Where

What

Who

Why

3 Practice

- Students write the questions. As they do so, ask them to think about a possible answer for each question.
- Check the questions with the class and elicit a range of possible answers.

Answers

2 What sort of food do aliens like?

3 What do they drink?

4 Who does the alien want to meet?

5 Why does he want to visit our planet?

6 Where does the Queen live?

7 When does the Queen eat her lunch?

4 Key pronunciation *Stress and intonation*

- Ask students to read the sentences and to predict where the main stresses fall in each sentence.
- 🔊 Play the recording once or twice. Students match the sentences with the stress and intonation patterns. Show the rising/falling intonation at the end with your hands.
- 🔊 Play the recording again. Students listen and repeat.

Answers

1 b 2 a 3 b 4 c

5 Writing and speaking *An interview*

- Explain the task and read out the question and answer. Choose a celebrity and elicit other questions that an interviewer could ask, using different question words.
- In pairs, students discuss which famous person they will choose for their interview and agree on their roles as the famous person and the interviewer.
- Students work together in their pairs to write the interview. Ask them to write at least three questions and answers. (The answers don't need to be true.)
- Pairs practise their interview. Encourage the 'famous people' to act their part as expressively as possible.
- Each pair joins up with another to read out their interview.
- You can invite some pairs to perform their interview for the class. Encourage other students to add their own questions at the end.

CHAPTER 3 The Silent Powers

The house in the trees

BACKGROUND

A **moonstone** is a pearly white semi-precious stone.

- Ask some true/false questions to revise previous events in the story. For example:
  - *Sophie's got a strange text message. (True)*
  - *Seth's cottage is called White Horse Cottage (False. It's called White Lady Cottage.)*
  - *Sophie has a dream about the White Lady. (True.)*
  - *The dog in Sophie's dream is brown, with strange yellow eyes. (False. It's black, with strange yellow eyes.)*
  - *Sophie wants to find a man called Mr Neil. (True.)*
- Focus on the picture and ask students what they can see.

- 🎙 Play the recording for the first paragraph (or read it out) while students listen and follow in their books. Use the picture to elicit the meaning of *wood* and *moonstone*.
- 🎙 Play or read out the rest of the story. Elicit or explain the meaning of new vocabulary (*silent, friendly, important, special powers, difficult* etc.).
- Choose a pair of students to take the parts of Sophie and the old man and ask them to read out the text as a dialogue. A third student can read the pieces of narration, or you could do this yourself.
- Ask these comprehension questions and elicit answers from the class. Alternatively, you could write them on the board and ask students to write down the answers.
  1 *Where is the old man's house? (In the wood near White Lady Cottage.)*
  2 *Does the old man know Sophie's age? (Yes, he does.)*
  3 *Does Sophie play the piano? (Yes, she does.)*
  4 *Does the old man answer her questions? (No, he doesn't.)*
  5 *What has he got for Sophie? (He's got a small white stone / a moonstone.)*
  6 *Why is the stone different from other stones? (Because it's got special powers.)*
  7 *Does the dog know where White Lady Cottage is? (Yes, he does.)*
  8 *When Sophie sees Cabal, what does she remember? (The dog in her dream.)*
- 🎙 Play the recording once more, while students follow in their books. Ask students what they think the moonstone's 'special powers' could be. How could it help when things are difficult? What difficult things could Sophie have to face? Discuss these questions in the students' language.
- Students could practise the dialogue between Sophie and the old man in pairs, leaving out the narration. Encourage them to say the lines as expressively as they can and to use appropriate actions (taking out the text message, handing over the moonstone, etc.). You could choose a pair to perform the dialogue for the class.

Puzzle tasks

- Students work individually on the puzzle tasks. You may choose to set them for homework.
- Students may need to refer back to Chapter 2 (page 41) for the answer to the first question.

> **Answer** Mr Neil.

- Explain the word *mirror* and tell the students to look at the word in mirror writing. Ask them to work out the word and explain what the word means.

> **Answer** gift

- For the last puzzle, revise the compass points if necessary. Students plot the moves on the grid to locate the position of Seth's cottage.

> **Answer** White Lady cottage is on square G:7.

Extra exercises

1
- Tell students to look carefully at the subject of each sentence to choose the correct answer.

> **Answers**
> 1 a 2 b 3 b 4 a 5 c 6 c

2
- Look at question 1 with the class. Remind students that if the question uses the verb *be*, the short answer must also use it. If the question uses any other present simple verb, the answer must use *do* or *does*.
- When you check the answers, emphasise the difference between *What does he like?* and *What's he like?*.

> **Answers**
> 1 b 2 c 3 c 4 b 5 a

3
- Students complete the matching task.
- After checking their answers, you can prompt them with other words to substitute in the questions. For example:
  1 *they (Do they believe in ghosts?)*
    she (Does she believe in ghosts?)
    she / aliens (Does she believe in aliens?)
  Elicit answers to these questions.

> **Answers**
> 1 f 2 d 3 a 4 b 5 e 6 c

4
- Read out the list of nouns a–i and check that students remember all the words.
- Students complete the matching task.

> **Answers**
> 2 h listen to music
> 3 g read English magazines
> 4 i write emails
> 5 b play hockey
> 6 d believe in UFOs
> 7 a speak two foreign languages
> 8 c wear a uniform
> 9 e drink coffee

5
- Students write one word in each gap.

> **Answers**
> 1 do 2 speak 3 Does 4 go 5 Why 6 Where

6
- Ask students to work on the translations in pairs or small groups, and then discuss with the whole class.

Extra reading

Schools

In all three countries, there is a range of types of secondary schools, both state-run and private.

In the UK, as in Australia, there are some specialist schools with an emphasis on a particular area such as music, information technology or the performing arts, as well as schools that cater for children with disabilities. However, in both countries these schools are a minority. Most secondary students attend broad-based, non-specialist schools.

In the UK and Australia, students are expected to take a number of different subjects in their junior years, and to study fewer subjects in greater depth when they are 16–18. In the USA, there is no such specialisation – students continue to study a range of subjects in their last two years of high school and in their early years at college (university).

American students are more likely to leave school at 16, while in the other two countries it is more common to stay on to the age of 18.

British and American schools often serve hot meals at lunchtime in the canteen or dining room. For those who bring their own food to school, a typical British packed lunch is sandwiches, crisps, cake or biscuits and fruit.

Lead in

- Ask students about their school.
- Look at the photos. Ask what students can say about the photos. Find out if students have any information or impressions about schools in the UK, Australia or the USA.

Task

- On the board, write the words used for the different levels of schooling in the three countries:

  kindergarten / nursery school / pre-school
  – children up to the age of about 5

  primary/elementary school
  – pupils from about 5 to 11 or 12

  secondary/high school
  – pupils from 11 or 12 to 18

- Choose students to read out the listed sentences 1–6. Students read the text to decide if the sentences are true or false. You could ask them to correct the ones that are false.
- Check the comprehension of any new words in the text, with the class.
- Invite students to discuss some of the differences between the schools in the text and their own school system. What do they think is a good age for children to start school? Would they like to study at home?

> **Answers**
> 1 True.
> 2 False. (They eat in the canteen or take a packed lunch.)
> 3 False. (Some students go to a special type of high school.)
> 4 True.
> 5 False. (They start when they're six.)
> 6 False. (They go to the senior prom when they're 18.)

6 I'm usually late!

Grammar: Present simple + frequency adverbs
Communicative task: Talking about habits

1 Presentation *Snakes never blink*

> **BACKGROUND**
>
> American grizzly **bears** are particularly skilful at fishing. In autumn they scoop up the salmon that are swimming up the rivers to spawn.
>
> A **giraffe**'s tongue (blue-black in colour) is up to 45 cm long. Giraffes can use their tongues to clean their noses as well as their ears
>
> **Snakes** don't blink because they have no eyelids. (This is also true of fish.)

a ● You could start by asking students to say the names of the animals in the photos. Introduce some of the new words from 1a and 1c here.
  ● Ask students to read the sentences and match them with the photos.
  ● 📻 Play the recording. Students listen and check their answers.
  ● Explain the new vocabulary and practise the pronunciation.
  ● Invite students to give any other interesting facts they know about these animals.

Answers 1 c 2 d 3 e 4 b 5 a

> **BACKGROUND**
>
> **Dolphins** sleep with one half of their brain at a time so they can keep one eye open to watch out for predators.
>
> There are 50 kinds of **sea snakes** in the Indian Ocean and western Pacific. They live on fish.
>
> For **gorillas**, the juicy fruit, leaves and stems of a rainforest diet, together with dew, usually provide all the water they need.
>
> **Lions** usually hunt at dusk, resting and sleeping during the day. Males let the females do most of the hunting for them.
>
> **Tarantulas** only attack humans if provoked. Their bite is usually no worse than a bee sting.
>
> **Dolphins** sometimes work together to attack a shark that is threatening the group.

> **Snakes** are much more dangerous to people than sharks – in fact, it has been estimated that snakes may cause up to 100,000 human deaths a year.
>
> **Bears** eat almost anything, including spiders, insects and lizards.

b ● Students look at the diagram to work out the meanings of the adverbs and translate them.
  ● Drill the pronunciation. Emphasise the first-syllable stress in all these words and draw attention to the silent *t* in *often*.
  ● Test comprehension by asking about the animals in 1a. For example: *Do bears <u>always</u> eat fish? (No, they <u>often</u> eat fish. They also eat meat, fruit and honey.) Do snakes <u>sometimes</u> blink? (No, they <u>never</u> blink. They can't close their eyes.)*

c ● Read out the sentences. Take some time to explain new vocabulary and to ensure that the meaning of the statements is clear.
  ● Students read the sentences again and guess whether they are true or false. They could exchange ideas in pairs or small groups.

Answers
1 True.   2 False.   3 True.   4 True.   5 False.
6 False.   7 True.   8 True.

2 Key grammar
Position of frequency adverbs

  ● Choose students to read out the two groups of examples. Draw attention to the difference in the position of the adverb. Students then complete the rule orally and/or in writing.

Answers before; after

3 Practice

a ● Students use the adverbs to write sentences about themselves.
b ● If they finish early, encourage them to use their own ideas to make more sentences.
c ● Students choose a sentence and scramble the words.
  ● In pairs, they re-order their partner's sentence without looking at their book.

4 Reading and listening *A questionnaire*

a ● Ask students to skim the questionnaire quickly. Ask: *Who is it for? How do you know?* Elicit or explain the meaning of *habit*.

- Focus on the new vocabulary: *on time, tidy, housework, exercise, lazy*. In most cases, the students should be able to guess the meanings from the context.

Answer b

b
- Make it clear to the students that they will hear Ben reading through the questionnaire and giving his answers.
- 🔊 Play the recording. Students listen and note down Ben's answers, a, b or c.
- Ask different students to say the sentences about Ben's habits. Remind them to use the *-s* or *-es* verb ending with *He*.

Answers

1 b 2 b 3 b 4 c 5 a 6 a
He sometimes tidies his room.
He sometimes helps with the housework.
He hasn't got a television.
He's often late.
He plays a lot of sport and he walks a lot.

Tapescript

Let's see … Number one: Homework.
a I always do my homework on time.
b I usually do my homework on time.
c I don't usually do my homework on time.
Er … *b*, I suppose. I usually do my homework on time. Two: Your room.
a I always tidy my room at the weekend.
b I sometimes tidy my room.
c I never tidy my room.
Well, I suppose I sometimes tidy my room, so it's *b* again. Three: Housework.
a I often help with the housework.
b I sometimes help at home.
c I never do any housework.
Oh … Well, I sometimes help with the housework – *b*. Four: TV.
a I always watch TV when I get home.
b I sometimes watch TV in the evening.
c We haven't got a television.
Well, that's easy. We haven't got a television. So it's *c*. Five: On time? Oh dear!
a I'm often late.
b I'm sometimes late.
c I'm not usually late.
I think that's *a*. I'm often late. Six: Exercise.
a I play a lot of sport and I walk a lot.
b I do PE at school but that's all.
c I'm lazy. I don't often get any exercise.
A, definitely *a* – I play a lot of sport and I walk a lot. So that's 1b, 2b, 3b, 4c, 5a and 6a.

c
- Students answer the questionnaire for themselves. Ask the class about some of their good and bad habits.

5 Speaking

a
- Go through the questions. Make sure that students know the meanings of all the words and drill the pronunciation. Note that *telly* is an informal abbreviation for *television*.
- You could invite the class to ask you the questions. When you answer, give explanations and use a variety of adverbs.

b
- Choose two students to read out the example dialogue. Elicit other possible answers for each question.
- In pairs, students ask and answer.

OPTION

Ask students to find all the adjectives in Exercises 3–5 and write them in two lists, *Positive* and *Negative*.
(*Positive*: energetic, helpful, well-organised
Negative: bored, late, lazy)

6 Writing *My habits*

- This writing exercise can be done in class or set for homework. Tell students to refer back to Exercises 4 and 5 for ideas, and encourage them to use frequency adverbs from the unit.

Example answer

I've got some good habits. I'm usually helpful at home and I often tidy my room. I'm not a telly addict and I get a lot of exercise. But I've got some bad habits too. I'm not very well-organised and I don't always do my homework on time.

Grammar: The verb *have*
Vocabulary: Food, drinks and meals
Communicative tasks:
  Talking about food and drink
  Writing a report about eating habits

STEP 2

1 Key vocabulary *Food and drink*

a
- Focus on the pictures and ask students which words they know in English. Many are likely to be familiar to them, and others may be similar to words in their own language.
- 🔊 Play the recording for students to listen and repeat. Pay special attention to the pronunciation of juice /dʒuːs/, yoghurt /ˈjɒɡət/, sausages /ˈsɒsɪdʒɪz/ and fruit /fruːt/.

- Invite the class to add any other English words they know for food and drink.

b
- Students write at least two sentences about their food preferences.
- Ask different students to say their sentences. Follow up with questions and encourage other members of the class to do the same. For example:

  A: I love chicken, but I never eat ham.

  B: Do you like sausages?

  A: No, I don't.

  📼 Pattern drill: TRP, page 12 (Unit 6, Step2).

2   Key pronunciation   *Vowel sounds*

a
- Ask students to read the words of the rhythm drill before they listen. Explain or elicit the meaning of *breakfast* and *dinner*.
- 📼 Play the recording. Students listen and follow in their books.
- 📼 Play the recording again, say the lines aloud and encourage the students to join in. Beat time or click your fingers to emphasise the rhythm.
- 📼 Play the recording line by line and ask students to repeat.
- You could divide the class into two halves, with one half asking the questions and the other answering. Then choose individuals to do the same. Make sure they keep up the rhythm.

b
- Say the six words and ask students to repeat. Pay particular attention to the diphthong /əʊ/ in *go* and the /ae/ sound in *bat*.
- Ask students to make six lists, selecting only the words for food and drink. Explain that when a word has two syllables, it's the vowel in bold type that they need to identify.
- 📼 Play the recording. Students listen and check their answers, You could ask them to add *breakfast* and *dinner* to the correct lists (/e/ and /ɪ/).
- Drill all the words in each group together.
- Draw attention to the /ə/ sound in the unstressed second syllable of *breakfast, salad, dinner* and *pasta*.

Tapescript/Answers

1   big, milk, chicken, fish
2   go, toast
3   see, tea, cheese
4   ten, eggs, bread
5   you   juice   fruit
6   bat   salad   pasta

OPTION

You may choose to teach the phonetic symbols for these vowel sounds. Tell students that it's useful to learn these for help with pronunciation, and remind them of the phonetic transcription of words in dictionary definitions.

Try this!

Answers

Words from the unit: meat, chicken, ham, steak, fish, bread, fruit, orange, milk, tea, lunch, snack

Some other words: lamb, bacon, salmon, tuna, salt, sugar, flour, rice, corn, cornflakes, cake, beans, garlic, herbs, mint, lemon, melon, lime, cola, cream

3   Reading and listening
A survey about food

a
- Focus on the photo. Ask students to identify the boy (*Joe*). Ask: *Where is he?* (*At a café.*) Tell them that the girl's name is Tamiko and ask them what they think she wants.
- 📼 Read out the question and then play the recording. Students listen with their books closed.

Answers

Breakfast, lunch and dinner.

b
- Students open their books and read through the dialogue. Ask them to try to remember or guess what the missing words are before they listen again.
- 📼 Play the recording once again. Pause after Joe's speeches to give students time to write. You could allow students to compare answers with a partner.
- Drill some of the questions and statements with *have*. Explain that we often use *have*, rather than *eat* or *drink*, when talking about food, drink and meals.
- You may also want to drill some of the useful expressions in the dialogue (*Is this seat free? What about lunch? That's all. Thank you very much. You're welcome.*)

Answers

1 toast   2 fruit juice   3 cereal   4 sandwiches
5 pizza   6 burger   7 meat   8 pasta   9 meat
10 vegetables   11 fish   12 crisps   13 Steak
14 chips

4   Reading   *Tamiko's report*

- Make it clear that the text is Tamiko's report on the results of her survey. Ask students to read the report to check their answers to 3b.
- Draw attention to the use of *has* with a third person singular subject (*he/she/it*).

OPTION

Focus on the phrase *a packet of crisps* and ask students to suggest other food items that come in packets. You could extend this to other types of containers. For example:

a packet of biscuits/sweets/tea/spaghetti

a box of cereal/eggs

a bottle of orange juice / water

a carton of milk/juice

I'm usually late!   51

5 Speaking

- Choose two students to read out the example question and answer.
- In pairs, students ask and answer.
- Invite several different students to report back to the class on their partner's meals. Remind them to use *has*, not *have*.

6 Writing *Food in my country*

- Ask the class to start planning their report, and give them any help they need with extra vocabulary. The writing can be completed for homework.

Example answer

I usually have bread, butter and jam with hot chocolate for breakfast. At lunchtime I often have sandwiches and fruit. When I get home from school, I have a packet of crisps or fruit. In the evening I usually have fish or chicken with salad or vegetables.

Some popular meals in my country are fish soup and grilled prawns.

STEP 3

Vocabulary:
The time
Vocabulary for daily routines
Communicative tasks:
Telling the time
Saying when people do things

---

1 Key vocabulary *The time*

a
- Look at the clock to remind students of the language used to tell the time. Write up some times in numerical form (for example, 11.00, 6.30, 9.15, 7.40, 1.10) and ask students to say them in words.
- If students are uncertain about times in English, revise more thoroughly by drawing a clock face on the board and drawing the hands in different positions. Start with hours, half-hours and quarter-hours before going on to the smaller time divisions.
- Set a time limit of five minutes. Students write the times as figures in chronological order. They could work on this in pairs.
- 🔊 Play the recording. Students listen and check their answers.

Tapescript/Answers

- two o'clock (2.00)
- quarter past two (2.15)
- twenty-five past two (2.25)
- quarter to three (2.45)
- five past three (3.05)
- twenty past three (3.20)
- twenty to four (3.40)
- ten to four (3.50)
- ten past four (4.10)
- half past four (4.30)
- twenty-five to five (4.35)
- five to five (4.55)
- five o'clock (5.00)

b
- Drill the question *What's the time?* and point out that the answer begins with *It's … .* Students answer using the real time.
- They can then draw a series of simple clock faces showing different times. In pairs, they ask and answer about the time on each clock.

2 Key vocabulary *Daily routines*

a
- Focus on the photo and use it to introduce *dive* and *diving champion*.
- Read out the introductory paragraph. Ask students to work out the meaning of the verb *train*.
- Give students time to look at the pictures of the things that Kitty does every day.
- Read out the sentences. Students work on their own to complete the matching task. If they aren't sure of some words, ask them to guess.
- As you go through the answers, establish the meaning of *get up, have a shower, leave, catch the bus* and *get to* (= arrive at). Read out the sentences again and ask students to repeat. Pay particular attention to the extra syllable in *catches* (but not in *leaves*).

Answers
1 i 2 d 3 f 4 b 5 g 6 h 7 c 8 a 9 e

b
- Ask students to guess the time for each activity. Encourage debate and discussion about this, and don't confirm or correct any answers at this stage.

3 Listening *Kitty's day*

a
- Ask students to write the numbers 1–9, corresponding to the sentence numbers in 2b. Explain that they need to write the time they hear for each activity.
- 🔊 Play the recording once through and then replay it, pausing after every second or third sentence to allow students time to write their answers.

- ▣ Play the recording once more. Students listen and complete or check their answers.

> **Answers**
> 1 5.30   2 6.00   3 7.30   4 8.20   5 8.25
> 6 8.50   7 4.15   8 7.00   9 8.30

Tapescript

I get up at half past five. Then at six o'clock I go to the swimming pool. I train for an hour and a half. At half past seven I have a shower and put my school uniform on. I usually have a drink and some cereal at the café before I go to school. I leave the swimming pool at twenty past eight and I catch the bus at twenty-five past. I get to school at ten to nine. I get home from school about quarter past four. I have a snack, and then I start my homework. We have our dinner about seven o'clock and I usually go to bed at half past eight.

b
- Get students to read out the example dialogue. Elicit the questions for the other eight activities.
- Emphasise the use of *does* in the questions and the *-s* verb ending in the answers.
- In pairs, students take it in turns to ask a question and to reply using their answers from 3a. If there is disagreement about the times, read out the correct answers.

  ▣ Pattern drill: TRP, page 12, (Unit 6, Step3)

4 Speaking   *My routines*

- Get two students to read out the example and give students time to write similar questions.
- In pairs, students ask and answer, recording their partner's times.

CHAPTER 4 The Silent Powers
The White Lady

- Ask students to name the three characters they have met in the story and to say what they remember about them. You could make notes on the board under the headings *Sophie Case*, *Seth Case* and *Mr Neil*.
- Draw attention to the chapter title and ask students to tell you anything they know so far about the White Lady.
- ▣ Focus on the first half of the chapter. Play the recording. (Alternatively, you could read the dialogue aloud.)
- Explain or elicit the meaning of *ride* and *go riding*.
- Ask these comprehension questions and elicit answers from the class.

1 *Is Sophie a bit scared of Mr Neil? (Yes, she is.)*
2 *Do dogs usually understand everything people say? (No, they don't.)*
3 *Who is Epona? (She's Seth's horse.)*

- It may be best if you read the second part of the chapter aloud yourself, as the language is a little more difficult (but you can play the recording if you prefer).
- Go over the last speech carefully, helping with key vocabulary: *signs, choose, mission, important, circle.*
- Continue with these comprehension questions for the second part of the text.

4 *Where does the strange white light come from? (From the moonstone.)*
5 *Who is the woman near the window? (The White Lady.)*
6 *When the Silent Powers need someone, what do they always do? (They write the person's name in the Book of Signs.)*
7 *Can Sophie talk to Seth about her mission? (No, she can't.)*
8 *Where is the Circle of Seven? (In Hunter's Wood.)*

- ▣ Play the recording once more, while students follow the story in their books.
- The Silent Powers have chosen Sophie for a 'mission'. Ask students what they think this mission could be. Is it going to be dangerous? What has she got to help her? Who seems to be on the side of the Silent Powers? What could the 'Circle of Seven' be – seven what? Discuss these questions in the students' language.
- If time, ask students to practise the two dialogues in pairs. Encourage them to say the lines as expressively as they can and to use appropriate actions. You could choose a pair to perform the dialogue for the class.

Puzzle task

- Students work individually to discover the words made up by the letters in the circle.

> **Answer:** a secret

Extra exercises

1
- Students fill in the names of the animals. If they aren't sure, tell them to look back to Step 1.

> **Answers**
> 1 dolphins   2 snakes   3 giraffes
> 4 tarantulas   5 bears

2
- Look at the example and note the position of the adverb, before the verb. Remind students that the adverb goes after the verb *be*.

3
- Elicit a possible answer for the example question.
- When students have completed the questions, they write their own answers.
- You can prompt the students with other words to substitute in the questions. For example:

  2 they   *(What do they usually have for breakfast?)*

  Anna   *(What does Anna usually have for breakfast?)*

  lunch   *(What do they usually have for lunch?)*

4
- Students read the questions and choose the correct replies.

5
- If students have any problems with the vocabulary here, refer them back to the relevant part of the unit.

6
- Ask them to work on the translations in pairs or small groups, and then discuss with the whole class.

Extra reading

My name is Dion

BACKGROUND

The first Australians were the Aborigines. Aboriginal people have been present in Australia for approximately 60,000 thousands years and today make up just over 1.5 per cent of the country's population. **Bidyadanga**, with about 600 residents, is the largest Aboriginal community in northwestern Australia. Tropical **cyclones** are not uncommon along this coast and in December 2000 a very dangerous category 5 cyclone, with winds of 280 km an hour, hit Bidyadanga. The authorities managed to evacuate everyone from the town before the cyclone arrived, except two people who refused to leave.

Lead in

- Find out if any students have a pen friend. Ask them to tell the class about their pen friend.
- Focus on the photos and ask students what they can say about them.

Task

- Read the questions aloud and check that students understand them.
- Students read the text, silently, to find the answers to the questions.
- Help with new vocabulary (*aboriginal, coast, cyclones, hot dogs*).
- Check answers with the whole class.

About Aboriginals

- Read out the short text in the About box. Ask students to tell you (in their own language, if necessary) anything else they know about Australian aboriginals.

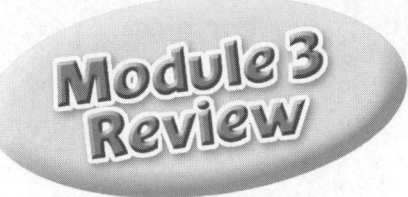

Language summary

1 Present simple

1.1 ● Students re-order the words to make sentences. Advise them to try to identify the subject of the sentence first, and then to look for the verb.

Answers
1 Mel and Barney live in Exeter.
2 I get up at seven o'clock.
3 Sadie goes to a judo club.
4 We eat a lot of crisps.
5 They watch TV every evening.
6 I clean my teeth every day.

1.2 ● Look at the example and ask students to make similar sentences, each beginning with *My friend Buzz*.
● Make sure that they have changed the pronoun from *my* to *his* in question 3, and that they have spelt *watches* correctly (NOT ~~watchs~~) in question 4.

Answers
2 My friend Buzz walks to school.
3 My friend Buzz does his homework before dinner.
4 My friend Buzz watches *Friends* on TV.
5 My friend Buzz helps with the housework.
6 My friend Buzz plays the guitar.

1.3 **Answers**
1 don't   2 doesn't   3 doesn't   4 doesn't   5 don't

1.4 ● Remind students of the order for questions:
Question word + *do/does* + subject + verb

Answers
1 Does, does   2 Do, do   3 do
4 Does, doesn't   5 Do, do   6 does

2 Frequency adverbs

● Make it clear that each sentence should start: *We (adverb) talk about* ... Remind them that adverbs go before the verb (except in the case of the verb *be*).

Example answers
We sometimes talk about food.
We don't often talk about (our) parents.
We often talk about clothes.
We sometimes talk about films.
We usually talk about music.

3 Telling the time

● Make it clear that there is one time in the second list that isn't there in the first one.
● When students have found the extra time (5.01), point out that we usually say this as *one minute past five* (NOT ~~one past five~~). We can also say *five oh one*.
● Referring to the first list, draw attention to the alternative ways of saying the quarter-hours and half-hours (*one fifteen, one thirty, one forty-five*). Elicit some other examples (for example, *half past two – two thirty, quarter to eight – seven forty-five*).
● You could go through the first list and ask students to say the alternative expression for all the other times (*five past one – one oh five, ten past one – one ten, twenty to two – one forty* etc.).

Answers
1.40 – twenty to two
1.10 – ten past one
1.30 – half past one / one thirty
5.01 isn't in the list.
1.55 – five to two
1.15 – quarter past one / one fifteen
1.45 – quarter to two / one forty-five
1.20 – twenty past one

4 *like* + noun

● If students have any difficulty remembering the words they need, tell them to consult the Vocabulary list or to look back at the relevant unit.

5 *have got* or *have*?

● Contrast the 'action' meaning of *have* with the 'owning' meaning of *have got*. Draw attention to the phrase *have a bath* and elicit the meaning.
● Remind students that the form is *has* for a third person singular subject (*he/she/it*).
● Point out that when we say *have/has got*, we often shorten *have* and *has* to *'ve* and *'s*. We can't do this when using the verb *have* on its own (*I have breakfast* – NOT ~~I've breakfast~~).
● You may want to tell students that in American English people don't use *have got* very often – they use *have* instead. So in American English we would use *have/has* for all the sentences in this exercise.

6 Expressions of time

- Read through the expressions in the box. Give students some other times and elicit the full expression, with the correct preposition. For example: *August (in August), half past nine (at half past nine), Saturday (on Saturday).*
- Go through the questions and make sure that students understand them.
- In pairs, students ask and answer.
- You can choose some students to report back on their partner's habits (for example, *Marek cleans his teeth in the morning and in the evening.*).

OPTION

For extra practice in structuring sentences using the present simple, frequency adverbs and expressions of time, ask students to experiment with a 'sentence machine'. Students cut a length of card, about 20 cm x 8 cm. Spaced out in a row in the centre of the card, they cut five 'windows'.

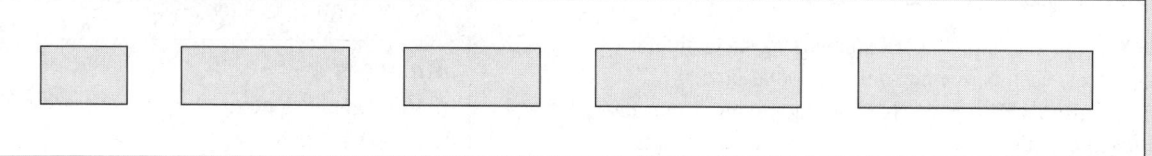

Then make five strips of card with sentence parts listed vertically, so that each part can be read through a 'window'.

1	2	3	4	5
I	always	play	football	at the weekend.
You	usually	see	(my) friends	after school.
We	often	go	TV	on Friday.
She	sometimes	watch	the guitar	at lunchtime.
Joe	never	plays	to the cinema	in the morning.
		sees	to school	
		goes		
		watches		

Students move the strips up and down behind the windows to make at least eight different sentences.

Study skills 3   How do you learn?

Here students are encouraged to think about their strengths and weaknesses and to consider things they can do for themselves to help them improve.

1
- Students read through the list and grade themselves on the eight areas of language learning.
- Ask them about the problem areas – what are the difficulties that they experience? Why do they find some activities easier than others? Invite them to discuss these questions (in their own language, if necessary). Encourage a range of views, to make students aware that while others share their experiences, individuals also have different strengths and different approaches to language learning. Invite them to talk about some of the strategies they use – both in class and when they are studying at home – to help them in the eight areas.

2
- Read through the sentences and explain or elicit the meaning of *web page* and *pen friend*.
- Ask students to make true sentences about themselves.
- Once again, discuss the outcomes. How could these home-based activities help with the areas listed in Exercise 1? If they already do some of these activities, what do they get out of them? Which others might be particularly helpful for them?

How's it going?

Your rating

- Students look back at the exercises in the Language summary and make their own assessment of how well they understand and remember the material. If their assessment is not very positive, are there approaches from Study skills that might help them to improve?

Vocabulary

- Students choose two titles from the Vocabulary list, then close their books. Students test their memory of the words they have learnt in these categories.

Test a friend

- Look at the example questions and elicit the correct answers. If students can't remember the information, ask them to look back over the module to find out.
- Students refer back to the texts in Units 5 and 6 and write several questions to test their partner. They then ask and answer in pairs.

Write to your teacher

- Use the students' letters to find out what they are enjoying and where they are having difficulties. Reply to the letters with a personal message in the students' language, giving help, praise and encouragement.

Your Workbook

- Students should complete the Learning diary when they come to the end of each unit.

Coursework   All about me!

A day in my life

Students write about:
- the beginning of their day
- their school routine
- the things they do after school

- Give students a few minutes to look at Jack's project about himself.
- Ask them to say what they can see in the pictures, and to identify Jack's bus pass and school timetable. Teach the English words for these, and introduce other key words (*nurse, wildlife, website* etc.).
- Give students a few minutes to read Jack's report. Then help with any new vocabulary. Help them to work out the meaning of the words in the timetable. (Note that *registration* isn't a subject – it's the time when the teacher marks the register to record which students are present and which are absent.) Invite students to make comparisons with the organisation of their own school day.
- Ask students to think about the way Jack's project is organised. Can they identify a topic for each paragraph? (Example answers: *paragraph 1: before school, 2: getting to school, 3: at school, 4: after school.*) You could ask them to use some or all of these topics to plan their text in an organised sequence of ideas. They should write three or four paragraphs and illustrate them as they wish.
- Set a time limit, allowing one or two weeks for work on the project. If students want to spend longer on this work, you could negotiate an extension of time. The work should be mainly done at home.
- Ask students to check their text before they copy it out and design their page. Tell them to use Jack's text as a model and remind them to look back at Units 5 and 6 if they need help with language.

Module 4

Inside and outside

See page 7 of the Introduction for ideas on how to use the Module opening pages

7 At home

Grammar: *There is/are, There isn't/aren't*

Vocabulary: Homes vocabulary

Communicative tasks:

Describing different rooms

Writing a description of your dream home

1 Key vocabulary *Homes*

- You might start by teaching or eliciting the meaning of *room*. Ask: *Where are we?* and elicit *We're in a classroom*. Write the word *classroom* on the board. Draw attention to its compound form (*class* + *room*) and to the stress on the first syllable.
- Focus on the picture of the house and ask students to see if they can match the words with the numbers in the picture.
- 🔊 Play the recording for students to check their answers and repeat the words.

Tapescript/Answers

1 upstairs
2 downstairs
3 bedroom
4 bathroom
5 toilet
6 shower
7 living room
8 hall
9 dining room
10 kitchen
11 garden

2 Presentation *There are 132 rooms*

The White House, the residence of the US President, is in Washington. There are 132 rooms on six levels, including offices for presidential staff. **The Oval Office** is the oval-shaped room where the President works, meets heads of state, and broadcasts important speeches on television.

Houseboats in Britain are often converted barges, just over 2 m wide and up to 22 m long, fitted out with sleeping, cooking and washing facilities. They are often hired out for holiday touring, but some people use them as homes.

- Look at the photos and ask students what they can see. You could also ask who they think lives in each home. Some students will probably recognise the White House as the US President's home, and others will recall Joe and Sadie's surname (Kelly) from previous units.
- Choose three students to read out the descriptions.
- Ask the class to suggest which picture matches each description and to give reasons. Don't confirm or correct the answers yet.
- 🔊 Play the recording. Students listen and check their ideas.
- You could ask them to repeat key phrases, for example: *There's a big living room, There isn't a dining room, There are three bedrooms, There aren't any bedrooms.*

Answers

1 The Kellys' house 2 The White House
3 A houseboat

3 Key grammar *There is/are*

- Choose students to read out the examples. Elicit the full form of *There's* (*There is*).
- Students complete the explanation orally and/or in writing.

Answers

there is, there isn't
there are, there aren't

4 Practice

a ● You can demonstrate by making a few statements about your own home. Then ask three or four students to do the same.

b ● Refer back to the information in Exercise 2, and read out the example dialogue.
  ● Students choose one of the homes and write a sentence, either true or false.
  ● In pairs, students read and respond.

5 Key pronunciation *Stress in sentences*

a ● 🎤 Play the recording while students follow in their books.
  ● Drill *There's _a* and *There isn't _a*, focusing on the sound links.
  ● Repeat the poem line by line. Beat time with your hand to show the stress, and encourage the students to do the same as they repeat.

b ● Students identify the stressed words. They then say the complete poem together. You could follow up with a further reading where different students or groups read a line each.

> ### Answers
> hill, sea;   hill, house;   house, room;
> small, white, door;   sign, door;   sign, ME;
> door, locked;   isn't, key

6 Writing *My dream home*

  ● This exercise can be done in class or set for homework. Make sure that students understand the meaning of *dream home* before they start.

> ### Example answer
> My dream home is a modern house near the sea. There's a beautiful living room, a dining room and a big kitchen. Upstairs there are five bedrooms. There are two bathrooms. There are big windows and lots of pictures in all the rooms. There's a swimming pool and a tennis court in the garden.

> ### Try this!
> **Answer:** The odd one out is *mushroom*. This is a type of food. The others are all rooms in a home.

> **Grammar:**
> *There's a/some … There are some …*
> *Is/Are there …?* + short answers
> Uncountable nouns
> **Communicative tasks:**
> Asking and answering about places and food
> Inventing some 'disgusting recipes'

1 Presentation *Is there any juice?*

a ● Ask students about the photos. Elicit the information that Kate is Sadie's older sister and establish that she lives on the houseboat.
  ● Ask students: *Would you like to live on the houseboat? Why / Why not?*

b ● Read out the introduction to the dialogue, or ask a student to do so. If you have a map of the UK, you could point out where Bristol is.
  ● 🎤 Read out the question. Remind students that Sadie is a vegetarian, and invite suggestions about the food she might want. Books closed, they listen for the answer.

> **Answer** She wants vegetable lasagne.

c ● 🎤 Play the recording again while students follow in their books. Pause to elicit or explain the meaning of new vocabulary.
  ● Ask questions to test comprehension, for example:
    Where does Kate sleep?
    Does she watch TV on the houseboat?
    Is there anything to drink?
    Has Kate got any pasta?
    Where are the girls going before dinner?
    Why does Kate want some paper?
  ● Choose students to read out the sentences. Ask them to find the place in the dialogue that shows whether the first sentence is true or false (*I've got a radio.*).
  ● Students decide if the sentences are true or false. Check the answers with the class.
  ● Read out the three questions in the dialogue with *Is/Are there*, and elicit the correct short answers: *Is there a television? No, there isn't*, etc. Then drill the questions and the answers.
  ● You may also want to drill some of the useful expressions in the dialogue (*I'm thirsty, I'm hungry, Here you are*).

> ### Answers
> 1 False. (There's a radio in the living room.)
> 2 True.
> 3 False. (There isn't any fruit juice.)
> 4 False. (There aren't any vegetables.)
> 5 False. (There's some paper on the desk.)

d • Give students a few minutes to find the items in the dialogue.

> **Answers**
> fruit/apple juice, vegetables, lasagne, milk, cheese

2 Key grammar
Is/Are there ...? + *short answers*

• Students give the correct verbs in the example questions and answers, orally and/or in writing.

> **Answers**
>
> | Questions: | Short answers: |
> | --- | --- |
> | Is | is |
> | | isn't |
> | Are | are |
> | | aren't |

3 Practice

• Focus on the classroom. In pairs, students ask and answer about the things in the list.

> **Answers**
> 2 Is there a television?
> 3 Are there any posters?
> 4 Is there a telephone?
> 5 Are there any computers?
> 6 Are there any cupboards?

🔊 Pattern drill: TRP, page 13, (Unit 7, Step 2, Drill 1.)

4 Reading and listening *Kate's shopping*

a • Introduce the new food words (*tomatoes, peppers, onions*) using, for example, pictures from a magazine. Pay special attention to the pronunciation of *onions* /ˈʌnjənz/.

• Students copy the list and complete it. They then answer the questions with *There are*.

> **Answers**
> (fruit) juice, milk, lasagne, cheese

b • 🔊 Introduce the recording and read out the question. Students listen for the answer.

> **Answer** She wants to buy some crisps.

Tapescript

KATE: OK. I've got the list. So ... vegetables. We need some onions. Here they are ... onions. Peppers ... Where are the peppers?

SADIE: Here. How many do you want?

KATE: Two. We want a green pepper and a red pepper.

SADIE: OK.

KATE: And we need some tomatoes.

SADIE: Tomatoes. Tomatoes ... Here you are.

KATE: Thanks, Sadie ... Right, we need some water and some milk.

SADIE: Don't forget the fruit juice.

KATE: Oh yes! You want some apple juice. Here it is. So we've got some apple juice, and some milk and some water.

SADIE: Don't forget the lasagne!

KATE: Oh yes, lasagne. The pasta's over there. OK ... so we've got a packet of lasagne.

SADIE: Is that everything?

KATE: No, we haven't got any cheese ... and we haven't got any bread ... and we need some mushrooms too.

SADIE: I'm hungry. Can we buy a packet of crisps?

KATE: Sure. They're over there. What sort do you fancy?

c • 🔊 Refer students to their copy of Kate's shopping list. Play the recording, pausing after *onions* to check that the task is clear.

• 🔊 Students number the other food items (2–10) and identify the ones that the girls haven't got at the end of the dialogue.

> **Answers**
> 2 peppers   3 tomatoes   4 water   5 milk
> 6 fruit juice 7 lasagne   8 cheese   9 bread
> 10 mushrooms
> They haven't got any cheese, bread or mushrooms.

5 Key grammar *Uncountable nouns*

• Read out the notes and focus on the examples with uncountable nouns. Make it clear that we can't say *two waters* or *three breads*, and draw attention to the use of *some* (not *a*) with these nouns.

• Students complete the explanation orally and/or in writing.

• You could ask them to find other examples of uncountable nouns in the dialogue on page 74 (*juice, lasagne, milk, cheese, paper*).

> **Answer** some; any

6 Practice

a • Check through the list with the whole class.

> **Answers**
> *Countable:* sandwich, eggs
> *Uncountable:* bread, ham, butter, cheese, pasta

b ● Students complete the sentences orally and/or in writing.

Answers
1 any   2 a, any   3 some, any   4 some, some

🔊 Pattern drill: TRP, page 13 (Unit 7, Step 2, Drill 2).

7 Speaking

a ● Refer students to the picture of the trolley. Choose two students to read out the dialogue before asking the class to practise in pairs.

b ● Students ask and answer in pairs using *Is/Are there any ...?*

8 Speaking *Disgusting recipes*

● Read out the ideas for disgusting recipes. Elicit one or two more ideas for recipes.

● Students write down their own horrible 'recipe', using dictionaries if necessary.

● They each read out their 'recipe' and the class votes on the most disgusting.

Example answers
My disgusting recipe is a milkshake. There's some cheese and there are some bananas (in it).
My disgusting recipe is a sandwich. There are some insects and there's some tomato ketchup (in it).

STEP 3

Grammar: Prepositions
Vocabulary: Things in a room
Communicative tasks:
    Saying where things are
    Describing a room

---

1 Key vocabulary *Things in a room*

● Point to the plan and explain that it is a plan of Sadie's bedroom.

● Compare the plan to the picture of the same room on the right. Students identify the numbered items by using the words in the plan.

● 🔊 Play the recording. Students check their answers and then repeat the words, paying particular attention to the pronunciation of *drawers* /drɔːz/, *shelves* /ʃelvz/ and *wardrobe* /ˈwɔːdrəʊb/.

● Ask students to cover the plan and focus only on the picture. Call out the numbers 1–11 in random order to elicit the correct words for the objects.

Tapescript/Answers
1 chest of drawers   2 mirror   3 shelves
4 chair   5 desk   6 wardrobe   7 rug
8 bed   9 table   10 clock   11 lamp

2 Key grammar *Prepositions*

● Use classroom objects (a book, a bag and a pen etc.) to further demonstrate the meaning of the prepositions. For example: *Where's the pen? (It's in/on/under the bag, it's between the bag and the book* etc.) Check understanding by asking for a demonstration of each preposition.

3 Practice

● Refer back to the picture of Sadie's room. Ask about several of the objects, for example, *Where's the lamp? (It's on the table. / It's next to the clock.)* Check students understand *on the left/right*.

● Students read the text and write the prepositions. Allow them to compare answers with a partner before you check with the whole class.

Answers
1 on   2 above   3 next to   4 on   5 next to
6 above   7 opposite   8 under   9 in front of
10 behind / next to

OPTIONS

1 You can use the picture for a guessing game. Ask a student to choose an object in the picture. The rest of the class has to ask *yes/no* questions to work out what it is, for example, *Is it on the right? Is it next to the wall? Is it in a corner?* This could also be done with objects in your classroom.

2 Prepositions can be used for a game of 'Noughts and crosses' (see Games, page 103). You could play a second round of the game by using some of the nouns from Exercise 1.

4 Writing and speaking *My room*

● Give students time to draw and label their plan and make it clear that they must not show it to their partner.

● Students listen to their partner's description and try to draw the room. Encourage them to ask questions if they need to.

● They then compare their drawings and discuss any differences between them.

● You could ask one or two students to report back to the class on their partner's room.

The Circle of Seven

- Ask some questions to revise the previous chapter of the story. For example:
  - *Who or what is Epona? (Seth's white horse.)*
  - *The White Lady said, 'We need your help'. How does she know that Sophie can help? (Because her name is in the Book of Signs.)*
  - *Where must Sophie go the next morning? (To Hunter's Wood.) When must she be there? (At 11 o'clock.) What is she looking for? (The Circle of Seven.)*
- 📻 Play the recording of Chapter 5 (or read it out if you prefer) while the students listen and follow in their books.
- Ask students to point to the following in the picture: *three paths, a white horse, a circle of seven stones, a piece of paper, a strange red light.* Explain the word *queen* and remind them of the phrase *Be careful.* Then choose students to read out the story again.
- Ask these comprehension questions and elicit answers from the class.
  1 *Is Sophie at the Circle of Seven at ten to eleven? (No, she isn't.)*
  2 *How many paths are there in front of her? (There are three paths.)*
  3 *How is the moonstone useful to her? (When she touches it, it gives her the answer to a problem.)*
  4 *What is the Circle of Seven? (It's a circle of seven stones.)*
  5 *What is there in the middle of the circle? (There's a piece of paper with a message.)*
  6 *Who is the message from? Can you guess? (It's probably from the Silent Powers.)*
  7 *Why is Epona important? (Because the Silent Powers need a white horse.)*
  8 *Who is dangerous? (The Red Queen is dangerous.)*
- 📻 To conclude, play the recording while students follow the story in their books.
- Invite students to guess why the Silent Powers need a white horse, and to predict what the 'strange red light' could be – is it something good or bad? What's going to happen next? Discuss these questions in the students' language.

Puzzle tasks

- Students work on the puzzle tasks individually. You may choose to set them for homework.
- Ask students to give a reason for their answer to the first puzzle.

Answer
It's the path in the middle (because the middle card is a seven and Sophie is looking for the Circle of Seven).

- For the second puzzle, students follow the clues to find the missing word in the wordsquare. If they have any trouble with the prepositions, tell them to look back to Exercise 2 on page 76.

Answer ANSWER

Extra exercises

1
- Remind students to look carefully to see if the subject is singular or plural before they fill in the gaps.

Answers
1 Are 2 Is 3 Is 4 Are 5 Is 6 Are

2
- Look at the noun that follows each gap in the exercise and ask: *Is it countable or uncountable?*
- Students complete the exercise individually or in pairs.

Answers
1 some 2 any 3 a 4 any
5 an 6 some 7 any

3
- Students read the questions and choose the correct replies.

Answers
1 b 2 c 3 a 4 b 5 a

4
- Point out that sentences 2, 4 and 6 are questions – the others are statements and end with a full stop. Remind students to use a capital letter at the beginning of each sentence.

Answers
1 There are some photos on the wall.
2 Is there a lamp on the desk?
3 There's a gym in the White House.
4 Are there any shelves in Sadie's room?
5 There's a mirror above the chest of drawers.
6 Is there a wardrobe in your bedroom?

5
- Read out the first sentence and elicit the correct answer. Note that we normally talk about being *on* a boat (although *in* is also sometimes used).
- When students continue, you can ask them to cover the alternatives below and to predict what the missing words will be as they read. They then look at the alternatives and choose the correct answers.

6
- Do the first few words with the class first, as examples.
- Students complete the lists. Allow them to compare lists with a partner before you check the answers.

7
- Refer back to the Step 2 dialogue to remind students of who said these expressions and in what situation. Make it clear that *Anyway* is a conversational 'filler', often used when we move from one subject to another.
- Ask students to work on the translations in pairs or small groups, and then discuss with the whole class.

- Students read the text to decide if the other sentences are true or false, or if we don't know because the answer isn't in the text.
- Check comprehension by asking a few questions, for example, *Who lives in a caravan? How many bedrooms are there in the Jones's house?* etc.
- Ask students which of the five homes in the text they would prefer to live in, and why.

Extra reading

Homes in the UK

BACKGROUND

About 90% of people in the UK live in urban areas. With over 7 million inhabitants, London is the city with the largest population, followed by Birmingham, Leeds, Glasgow, Sheffield, Manchester and Liverpool.

The number of people in rented accommodation is low in comparison with most other European countries. Almost 70% of UK households live in homes that they own. The British also prefer to live in houses – only 15% of British households live in flats.

Lead in

- Look at the photos and discuss the question with the class. Introduce some of the key vocabulary for the reading text at this stage (*semi-detached/terraced house, flat, cottage, caravan*) and establish the differences between these types of homes. Ask for students' ideas about whether most British people live in cities/towns or in the country, and what kind of homes they live in.

Task

- If you have a map of the UK, point out the location of Edinburgh and remind students that it is a large city, the capital of Scotland. Also point out where Leeds is.
- Look at the first true/false sentence and ask students to find the place in the text that shows if the sentence is true or false.

Grammar: *can/can't* for abilities

Vocabulary: Verbs that describe abilities

Communicative tasks:

Talking about abilities

Making a notice for a club

1 Key vocabulary *Abilities*

- Read out the words and phrases in the list.
- Set a time limit of three minutes and ask students to match the words with the pictures. They could work on this in pairs. A lot of the words should be familiar already or easy to guess.
- 📻 Play the recording. Students check their answers and repeat the words.

Tapescript/Answers

1	dance	7	draw
2	sing	8	ski
3	swim	9	dive
4	speak Chinese	10	play the guitar
5	play football	11	stand on my head
6	cook	12	ride a horse

2 Presentation *Yes, I can!*

a
- Explain the word *abilities* in the students' language. They then read the lines of the song and count the abilities.
- Elicit the meaning of *I can* and drill the phrases with *I can* + verb. Pay attention to the schwa sound in the unstressed form of *can* /kən/.

> **Answer** Four.

b
- Invite students to suggest more words from the song, using the verbs in Exercise 1.

3 Listening *Song*

a
- 📻 Play the song. Allow students to enjoy listening to it and to pick up what they can.
- Ask the question and elicit the answer. Focus on the word *can't* and elicit the full form (*cannot*).

> **Answer** He can't dance.

b
- Choose students to read out the sentences and ask the class to repeat. Invite students to say which of these they think they heard in the song.

- 📻 Play the song again. Students decide if the sentences are true or false, or if we don't know because the actions aren't mentioned.
- 📻 Ask them to turn to the song words on page 144. Play the song once again and encourage them to join in.

> **Answers**
> 1 We don't know. 2 False. 3 False.
> 4 True. 5 We don't know.

4 Key grammar *can/can't*

- Refer back to the sentences with *He* in 3b. Draw attention to the fact that the form of *can* and *can't* doesn't change.
- Students complete the table orally and/or in writing.
- Focus on the question and short answer forms. Remind students that we don't use *do* or *does* here.
- Prompt the students with other words to substitute in the questions. For example:

  she/swim   (*Can she swim?*)

  they   (*Can they swim?*)

  play the guitar   (*Can they play the guitar?*)

  Nod or shake your head after each question to elicit short answers (*Yes, she can. No, they can't.* etc.).

> **Answers**
> can
> can't

To extend the range here, you could write down verbs / verb phrases for abilities (some from Exercise 1 and some new ones) on slips of paper and put them in a bag. For example:

play the guitar	*stand on one foot*
play the drums	*speak English*
play volleyball	*speak French*
play tennis	*cook*
ride a horse	*swim*
ride a bike	*use a computer*
ride a skateboard	*use a mobile phone*

Invite different students to take out a piece of paper, read it and then mime the action for the rest of the class to guess. When students suggest an answer, they use *He/She can …* .

5 Practice

- Ask two students to read out the example dialogue. Choose others to ask and answer similar questions across the class.
- 🔊 Optional pattern drill: TRP, page 13, Unit 8, Step 1).

6 Speaking

a
- In pairs, students ask about each other's abilities. Encourage them to think of new questions to ask, as well as the ones they have been practising. Also encourage them to give a little more information in their answers than just *Yes, I can* or *No, I can't*.

b
- Choose several students to report on their partner's abilities.
- You can ask some quick follow-up questions to the whole class, out of interest, for example:
  Who can speak German/French? Who can ride a horse? How many people can swim five kilometres? etc.

7 Reading *The Champion Birdman*

The Bognor Birdman contest is held every year at the resort town of Bognor Regis. The entrants, dressed in amazing costumes and home-made flying apparatus, leap off the end of the pier, hoping to win a prize of £25,000 by travelling 100 metres (without any form of aircraft or engine) before dropping into the sea. So far the furthest anyone has got is 89.2 metres in 1992. Around 40,000 people come to watch the event and the money raised goes to charity.

Bognor Regis is on the Sussex coast between Brighton and Portsmouth.

a
- Ask students to look at the photos and the caption with them. Introduce the words *competition* and *competitors* and ask students what they think the Birdman Competition is. Elicit or teach the key words *fly* and *wings*, using the photos.
- 🔊 Read out the question and then let students read the article quickly to find the answer.

Answer He can fly 44 metres.

b
- Read out the questions. Drill the pronunciation of *competition* and *competitor*, emphasising the difference in stress. Students read the text again and write their answers to the questions.

- You may want to point out that in this text *can* is sometimes used to express possibility (*You can see a flying horse, You can get more information*) as well as ability (*People can't fly, The Champion Birdman can fly 44 metres*). *Can* for possibility is taught more fully in Step 2.

Answers
1 Every year in August.
2 In Bognor, on the south coast of England.
3 A flying frog, an elephant with very big ears and a man with wings.
4 Yes, there are.
5 Yes, there is.

c
- Students answer the questions, then demonstrate the things that they can do. For question 4 you could invite several students to come to the board and do a quick Birdman drawing for the class.

8 Writing *A notice for a club*

- Look at the notice with the class. Ask students what they think it is and who it is for. What sort of group is the Westover Drama Club?
- Make sure that everyone understands the meaning of *join* (= *become a member*).
- Elicit a few suggestions for other clubs which could advertise in this way (for example, a music club, a camera club, an art club, a sports club).
- Students each decide on a club and write the text for their notice. They could complete the notice for homework, adding illustrations if they wish. You could have a class vote on the most eye-catching notice.

Try this!
Answers: A mosquito, a plane, a bat, a bird and a fly can fly. A horse and a chicken can't fly.

Grammar:
  can for possibility
  can + see/hear
Vocabulary: Places in a town
Communicative tasks:
  Talking about things you can do in your town
  Describing sights and sounds

STEP 2

1 Key vocabulary *Places in a town*

a
- Focus on the map and tell the class that it is the city centre of Exeter. Look at each of the labelled places and ask students to explain the words by giving local/well-known examples of these places.

- ● 🔊 Play the recording for students to listen and repeat the words.
- ● Ask for any other words they may know for places in a town (*shop, supermarket, theatre, art gallery, hospital, police station, football ground* etc.).

b
- ● Invite students to make sentences using the vocabulary from 1a.

2 Presentation *You can visit the aquarium*

a
- ● Look at brochure of Exeter. Read out the instruction and the question.
- ● Read out the text and ask students if, they think Exeter is an interesting town. Elicit or explain the meaning *visit* and *surf the Net*. Draw attention to the expressions with *go + -ing*. You could explain that it's possible to say *You can go walking* also, but this refers to a long trek (for example, in the countryside or in the mountains) rather than a stroll in the park.
- ● Point out that in these sentences *You* is used not to address a particular person but to mean 'People in general'. Ask students to say how this can be translated in their language.

OPTION

You might want to introduce some other expressions for activities with go, for example:

go ...ing	*go for a ...*
go skiing	*go for a swim*
go riding	*go for a ride*
go dancing	
go surfing	

b
- ● Drill the questions.
- ● Students ask and answer the questions about Exeter, referring to the map. Tell them that some questions may have more than one answer. Encourage them to add more questions of their own (*Where can you catch a train/bus / go bowling / go for a walk / play basketball?* etc.).
- ● Choose students to ask and answer across the class.

> **Example answers**
> 2 At the sports centre. / At the Internet café / In the park.
> 3 At the sports centre. / In the park.
> 4 At the Internet café.
> 5 At the aquarium.
> 6 At the museum.

3 Key grammar can *for possibility*

- ● Discuss the best translation for each sentence with the class.

4 Practice

a
- ● Students refer to the map and write sentences about other activities that are possible in Exeter.

> **Example answers**
> You can catch a train at the station.
> You can catch a bus at the bus station.
> You can buy food and clothes at the shopping centre.
> You can play basketball at the sports centre.
> You can see some interesting fish at the aquarium.

b
- ● Invite students to talk about the possibilities in their town. You can expand this into a general discussion about facilities which are available or which students think the town needs.

5 Presentation *I can hear the traffic*

a
- ● Students look at the map to find Barney's flat.

b
- ● Focus on the photos and ask students to say what they can about the location of the flat and about Barney's room.
- ● Introduce the verb *hear* and ask: *What can Barney see and hear in the morning? What do you think?* Invite students to suggest their ideas. You could introduce the word *traffic* here.
- ● 🔊 Play the recording at least twice. With books closed, students listen and write down the things that Barney can see and hear.

c
- ● Ask students to read the text to check their answers. Make sure that they understand the meaning of *wake up* and *look (out of the window)*.

> **Answers**
> He can hear his brother's radio, his mum and dad, the traffic and sometimes a train.
> He can see the wardrobe, his posters, the shops and houses opposite, some trees and the park.

6 Key grammar can + see/hear

- ● Discuss the best translation for each sentence with the class. Remind students that after *can* and *can't* we always use the infinitive of the main verb (without *to*).

7 Practice

a
- ● You could ask students to close their eyes for a few moments and imagine that they are in their room in the morning. They then write their answers. Ask a few students to read out their answers.

b   ● Choose students to read out the dialogue and ask the class to suggest possibilities for the word beginning with d (*door, desk, dress, dictionary* etc.).

   ● In pairs, students play the guessing game.

   🔊 Pattern drill: TRP, page 13 (Unit 8, Step 2).

8 Key pronunciation *can/can't*

   ● 🔊 Ask students to read the sentences first. Then play the recording. Students listen and repeat.

   ● Emphasise the difference in sound between the stressed and unstressed forms of *can*.

   ● You may want to tell the class that in American English the words *can't* and *dance* are pronounced with the /ae/ sound.

9 Writing and speaking *An amazing view*

   ● Look at the photo and explain the phrase *an amazing view*.

   ● Read out the instruction. Tell students to decide on the location of their building (it can be real or imaginary) and to try to visualise the things below them. Ask them to jot down notes as they think of ideas.

   ● Using their notes, students write their description.

   ● Ask some students to read out their description to the class.

STEP 3

Grammar:
   must/mustn't
   Imperative (revision)
Communicative task: Telling people what to do

1 Presentation *You mustn't argue*

a   ● Look at the photo and ask students to identify the people (Sadie and her father).

   ● Make it clear that they are having an argument about television. Read out the questions and explain that *Top of the Pops* is a pop music programme for a teen audience.

   ● 🔊 With books closed, students listen to the dialogue.

   ● Ask: *Mr Kelly gives some different reasons – what are they?* Students may be able to identify one or more of these before they listen again.

b   ● 🔊 Play the recording again while students listen and follow in their books. Ask them to say what Mr Kelly is telling Sadie to do.

   ● Students put the sentences in order. Check answers.

   ● 🔊 Play the recording once again. Pause after each part of the argument and drill the sentences with *must/mustn't*.

   ● You may also want to drill some of the useful expressions in the dialogue (*It's in a mess. What's the problem? Don't be rude!*).

   ● You could point out that there is another use of *can* and *can't* in this dialogue. When Sadie asks *Can I watch ...?* she is asking for permission, and when her father says *No, you can't* he is refusing permission.

2 Key grammar *must/mustn't*

   ● Ask students to translate the sentences into their own language and ask how they express *must/mustn't*. Is it similar or different in their language?

   ● Point out that the form of *must/mustn't* is similar to *can/can't*. They are followed by the infinitive (without *to*) of the main verb, and we don't use any form of *do*.

   ● You could give some examples with different subjects to make it clear that the form of *must/mustn't* doesn't change. For example: *Sadie must go to school tomorrow. We mustn't forget Dad's birthday on Tuesday.*

3 Practice

a   ● Students complete the sentences orally and/or in writing.

   ● Ask them to suggest some other examples of things that adults tell teenagers to do, using *must* and *mustn't*.

Having fun   **67**

b
- In pairs, students practise the dialogue. They may be able to think of other things for Mr Kelly to say, for example: *You must help with the dinner / clean your shoes / finish your art project.*
- 🔊 Pattern drill: TRP, page 13, (Unit 8, Step 3).

4 Reading *A poem*

a
- Read out the question and explain the meaning of *adult*. Students read quickly to find the answer.

> **Answer** A teenager.

b
- Go through the poem line by line, helping with new vocabulary. Ask students to suggest situations for each of the things that the adults say.
- Use the Remember! box to revise imperatives if necessary. Emphasise the use of *Don't* in the negative form.

> You could put the students into groups (three per group is an ideal number) to practise the poem. They can read the first line together and then take turns, each reading a different 'adult' for each line after that. They read the last line together. Encourage them to read expressively, and choose one or two groups to 'perform' the poem for the class.

5 Writing *My poem*

- In pairs, students write their own poem. They can use some of the expressions from the book, but should also add others of their own (for example, *You must listen to me. You mustn't interrupt.*). They can use their dictionaries to find new vocabulary.
- Ask several pairs to read out their poem for the class.
- If possible, display the students' poems in the classroom

CHAPTER 6 The Silent Powers
Devil's Bridge

- Remind students of previous events. Read out some quotes from different characters and ask: *Who said this?* For example:
  - *'I am your guide – not here, but in another world.'* (The White Lady, in Sophie's dream)
  - *'This is a moonstone. It's got special powers.'* (Mr Neil)
  - *'That old man knows my name, my age, my birthday and my cat's name!'* (Sophie)
  - *'You can ride my horse. She's called Epona'.* (Seth)
  - *'Don't be scared, Sophie. We need your help.'* (The White Lady)
  - *'Come on, Epona! This is the right path.'* (Sophie)

- Ask students to say what happened in Chapter 5.
- 🔊 Play the recording for the first part of Chapter 6 (or read it out if you prefer) and focus on the message on the computer screen. Elicit or explain the meaning of *devil* and *bridge*.
- Ask students to look at the picture and to guess who the woman is. What does she want?
- 🔊 Play the rest of the chapter (or read it out) and help with key vocabulary (*move, impossible, voice, belong to, flash, silver, alone*).
- Ask: *Who does Sophie hear as a voice in her head?* (*Probably the White Lady.*)
- Choose students to take the parts of Sophie, the Red Queen and the White Lady, and ask them to read out the text as a dialogue. A fourth student can read the pieces of narration, or you could do this yourself.
- Ask these comprehension questions and elicit answers from the class. Alternatively, you could write them on the board and ask students to write down the answers.
  1. *What can Sophie see on the computer screen? (A message.)*
  2. *To find Devil's Bridge, who must Sophie do? (She must go to Hunter's Wood and follow the river for about a kilometre.)*
  3. *When she gets to the bridge, what can she see? (A tall woman with long dark hair.)*
  4. *What is the problem when Sophie looks into the Red Queen's eyes? (She can't speak and she can't move.)*
  5. *What does the Red Queen want? (The moonstone.)*
  6. *What mustn't Sophie do? (2 things) (She mustn't listen to the Red Queen or look into her eyes.)*
  7. *When can Sophie speak again? (When she looks at the moonstone.)*
  8. *The Red Queen can't stay with Sophie on the bridge. Why? (Because Sophie is using the moonstone.)*
- 🔊 Play the recording once more, while students follow the story in their books. Ask students why the meeting on the bridge was a 'test' for Sophie? Did she pass it? Why does the Red Queen want the moonstone? Discuss these questions in the students' language.
- Ask students to practise reading the scene at Devil's Bridge in groups of three, without the narration. The people reading the parts of Sophie and the Red Queen should use appropriate actions and expressions.
- Invite groups to act out the scene for the class.

Puzzle task

- Students work individually to discover the coded word. (The numbers refer to the position of the letters in the alphabet: A = 1, B = 2 etc.)

> **Answer** test

Extra exercises

1 ● Tell students the words are names of places in a town.

Answers
2 bus station   3 aquarium   4 Internet café
5 park   6 shopping centre

2 ● You could add some other questions, for example: *Where can I see a dinosaur / go bowling / get some exercise?*

Answers
2 At the aquarium.   3 At the Internet café.
4 At the shopping centre.   5 At the bus station.
6 At the park.

3 ● Remind students that the form of *can* remains the same for different subjects.

Answers
2 Can, use   3 Can, play   4 Can, ride
5 Can, swim   6 Can, cook   7 Can, see

4
Answers
a 2   b 7   c 3   d 4   e 1   f 6   g 5

5 ● As you check the answers, elicit an example sentence for some of the alternative words.

Answers
1 a   2 c   3 b   4 c   5 a

6
Answers
2 a   3 e   4 b   5 f   6 d

7 ● Tell students that all the verbs here are imperatives.

Answers
1 Be   2 Close   3 wash   4 tidy   5 Go

8 ● Ask students to work on the translations in pairs or small groups, and then discuss with the whole class.

Extra reading

Stephen Hawking

BACKGROUND

Since the early 1960s, the eminent physicist and mathematician Stephen Hawking has suffered from a progressive and incurable motor neuron disease that affects his muscle control and confines him to a wheelchair. In 1985 an attack of pneumonia required an operation on his throat which took away his power of speech. He communicates by means of a computer and speech synthesiser. Stephen Hawking is engaged by fundamental questions: the laws that govern the universe and the way it began. He has written extensively on relativity, gravity and quantum theory, with a particular interest in black holes. He is a professor at Cambridge University and has received dozens of awards and honorary degrees for his contribution to theoretical physics.

Lead in

● Look at the photo and discuss the question. Introduce some key words: *disease, wheelchair, nurse, secretary.*

Task

● Ask students to read the text themselves and to make a note of the words they don't know.

● Ask them to discuss the words in pairs and to try to work out their meaning from the context. Check the meaning of the new vocabulary.

● Students work individually to answer the questions.

● You can ask some more questions to test comprehension, for example:
  – *How do we know that Stephen Hawking is a very intelligent man? (He's a professor of Mathematics at Cambridge University.)*
  – *He can't talk – so how can he teach? (He uses a special computer to communicate.)*

● Ask students if they know of any other famous people who have overcome difficulties in order to be successful.

Answers
1   The UK / Britain.
2   He's got a neuromuscular disease.
3   Because he needs help to dress, eat and wash.
4   A special computer.
5   Mathematics.
6   He dictates his ideas to a secretary.

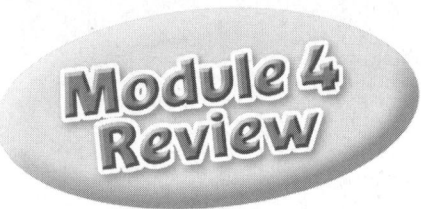

Language summary

1 There is/are

1.1 ● Students write their own answers for these questions.

1.2 ● When students have written the questions, allow them to discuss the answers in pairs.

● Pairs could also work together on some more general knowledge questions (these could include questions about their town/school) or questions based on information from texts in the Student's Book. Each pair then joins up with another pair to ask and answer.

Answers
2 Is there (Yes, there is.)
3 Are there (Yes, there are.)
4 Is there (Yes, there is.)
5 Are there (No, there aren't.)
6 Is there (Yes, there is / No there isn't.)

2 Countable and uncountable nouns

● Students complete the lists. You could ask them to add phrases using prepositions of place (*There's a sandwich in my bag. There are some tomatoes on the table. There's some milk in the fridge.*)

Answers
Singular: There's an egg, an apple, a sausage, an omelette
Plural: There are some sandwiches, onions, vegetables, bananas, chips
Uncountable: There's some bread, pasta, cheese, coffee, milk, fruit, orange juice, water

3 Prepositions of place

● Students make true sentences about things in the classroom. Check their answers with the whole class.

4 can

4.1 ● Collect suggestions and write them on the board. Help with vocabulary where needed.

Example answers
1 Bears can run / swim / climb / catch fish. Bears can't fly / talk / live under water.
2 A small baby can kick / smile / drink milk.

A small baby can't walk / talk / sit up.
3 Dolphins can swim / jump out of the water / communicate. Dolphins can't fly / live on land / stay under water.
4 Birds can fly / dive / catch insects / lay eggs. Birds can't live/fly under water.

4.2 ● Encourage students to use their imagination.

Example answers
I can walk under the chairs / ride on my dog / sleep in a drawer. I can't ride my bike / open the door.

4.3 ● Students use a verb from the first list and a word or phrase from the second one.

● As you go through the answers, ask students to say who the question could be addressed to and in what situation. Elicit some possible answers to the questions.

Answers
Can I watch TV?
Can I have a sandwich?
Can I go to Jack's house?
Can I play your guitar?

5 must

● Again, ask students to suggest who is speaking and who they are speaking to.

Answers
1 must 2 mustn't 3 mustn't 4 must
5 mustn't

6 there, they're and their

● Ask students to give the full form of *they're* and to translate *their*.

Answers
1 their 2 They're 3 There

7 Imperative

● Students match the two parts of the sentences.

Answers
Don't be rude.
Come to the cinema with us.
Listen to this song.
Don't sit in front of me.

Study skills 4 Learning vocabulary

- Encourage students to choose the method that they think will help them to remember the words best.
- If your students are already familiar with word maps, you could ask them to refine the categories and use a few more words. For example:

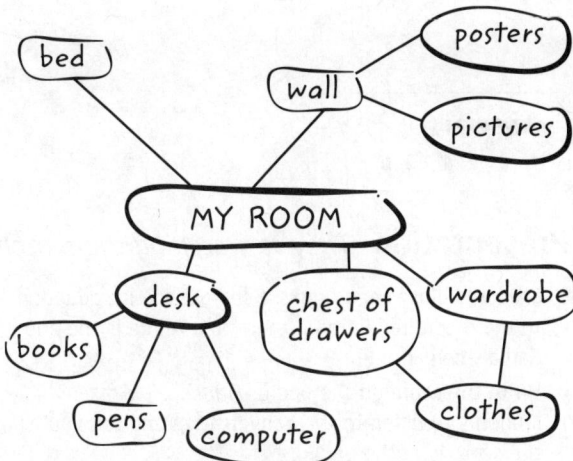

How's it going?

Your rating

- Students look back at the exercises in the Language summary and make their own assessment of how well they understand and remember the material.

Vocabulary

- Students test their memory of the words they have learnt in two of the vocabulary categories.

Test a friend

- Look at the example questions and elicit the answers.
- Students refer back to the texts in Units 7 and 8 and write questions about them to test their partner. They then ask and answer in pairs.

Write to your teacher

- Use the students' letters to find out what they are enjoying and where they are having difficulties. Reply to the letters with a personal message in the students' language, giving help, praise and encouragement.

Your Workbook

- Students should complete the Learning diary when they come to the end of each unit.

Coursework   All about me!

My neighbourhood

Students write about:

- places near their home
- things they do in these places

- Focus on the title of the project and elicit or explain the meaning of *neighbourhood*.
- Give students a few minutes to look at Jack's project about his neighbourhood.
- Ask them to say what they can see in the pictures.
- Ask students to read the text, and find out why these places are important to Jack.
- Invite students to identify a few of the places that are important to them in their neighbourhood.
- Ask students to choose their places and plan their text. They should write about at least four places and illustrate their paragraphs as they wish.
- Set a time limit, allowing one or two weeks for work on the project. The work should be mainly done at home.
- Ask students to check their text before they copy it out and design their page. Tell them to use Jack's text as a model and remind them to look back at Units 7 and 8 if they need help with language.

9   At the moment

STEP 1

Grammar: Present continuous: *Wh-* questions; affirmative

Communicative task: Talking about things in progress at the moment

1   Listening   *And it's a goal!*

BACKGROUND

The FIFA **World Cup** is the world's largest single sporting event. Over 200 countries participate in the qualifying rounds, from which 32 teams go through to the final contest, held every four years. In 2002, the World Cup in Japan and Korea had a cumulative TV audience of 28.8 billion worldwide.

a ● 🔊 Make sure that students keep their books closed while you play the recording. Ask them: *What's on TV?*. Introduce the words *final*, *match* and *goal*.

Answer

A football match (the World Cup Final).

Tapescript

… and Alain le Blanc has got the ball, and it's Le Blanc to Colombain … oh … and it's a goal! A goal for France! France have got another goal! So that's three all – three goals all in the World Cup Final! And the manager of Brazil is not a happy man. But what a fantastic final! A billion people are watching this match on television … a billion people are watching the World Cup Final today … So it's three all … and Brazil have got the ball, it's Marcos … Marcos to Silvio … Can they score again?

b ● Students now open their books. Read out the questions or choose students to do so. Make sure that students recognise the difference between *million* and *billion*, and establish the meaning of *score* and *three all*.

● 🔊 Play the recording again and ask students to answer the questions.

● Explain that *score* can be used as a noun (= the number of points in a game) or as a verb (as in *score a goal*).

Answers

1 b   2 a   3 b

2   Presentation   *They're watching the match*

a ● Students close their books. Read out the introduction to the recording. Remind them that Annie is Joe and Sadie's cousin.

● Write the score on the board: *France 3 – Brazil 3*. Ask students to listen to the conversation and tell you what the score is at the end.

● 🔊 Play the recording. Students listen and work out the score.

● Ask them to tell you which team scored the goal, and to add any information they picked up about who is watching the match.

Answer   Brazil 4 – France 3.

b ● 🔊 Play the recording again while students listen and follow in their books.

● Elicit the meaning of key words (for example, *scarf, support, Hang on*).

● Focus on the present continuous verbs in the dialogue and drill these sentences. Then read out the questions and elicit the answers, helping students with the form of the verbs.

● Ask some other comprehension questions, for example: *Is Annie watching the match in Australia? (Yes.) Why is Mr Kelly wearing green and yellow? (Because he's supporting Brazil.)*

● With a strong class, get students to ask and answer the questions in pairs.

Answers

1   They're watching the World Cup Final.
2   A green and yellow scarf.
3   Next to Mr Kelly.
4   Because Joe's supporting Brazil and Sadie's supporting France.

3 Key grammar *Present continuous:* Wh- *questions; affirmative*

- Read out each question, ask students to repeat and then elicit the answer. Ask for the full form and the short form (*I am* / *I'm*, etc.).
- Add questions to elicit answers with *We* and *You*, for example:

  Silvana and Leo, what are you doing now? (We're sitting in the classroom.)

  Where am I standing now? (You're standing behind the table.)

- Make sure students understand that the present continuous is used here for actions happening now, at the time of speaking. You can contrast this with the present simple, for example:

  I'm wearing my scarf (= I'm doing it now.)

  I wear my scarf when I go to the football (= this is something I do normally/regularly.)

- You could draw attention here to the spelling rules when we add an *-ing* ending (see page 142 in the Student's Book).

> **Answers**
> I'm
> She's
> They're

4 Practice

a
- Remind students to look carefully at the subject of the sentences when they form their questions.

> **Answers**
> 2 What are you doing?
> 3 Where is/'s Mr Kelly sitting?
> 4 Where are you sitting?
> 5 What are Joe and Sadie watching?

b
- In pairs, students ask and answer.

  📻 Pattern drill: TRP, page 14, (Unit 9, Step 1).

OPTION

You can use the photo on page 94 to ask some more present continuous questions. For example:

What's Joe wearing?

Where's Annie watching the match?

Where are Joe and Sadie sitting?

Which teams are playing?

Which team is winning?

5 Reading and speaking *The World Cup*

BACKGROUND

To calculate time in different parts of the world, the earth's surface is divided up into 24 **time zones**. The Greenwich Meridian, an imaginary line of longitude passing through Greenwich, is taken as the starting point. Each zone going west from here is one hour behind the last, and each zone going east is one hour ahead.

The time difference between England and Sydney varies, depending on when each of these countries turns the clocks back an hour for 'summer time'.

a
- Ask students to read the text and answer the question in 5a. Elicit the answer.

> **Answer** No. (5.6 billion people aren't watching the match.)

b
- Read out the two sentences under the map and if necessary, explain more about time zones (in the students' language if you wish).
- Look at the photos. Help the students to identify each of the countries for the cities, and ask: *What's the time in ...?*
- Drill the example dialogue and elicit one or two questions and answers for other cities.
- You could point out that normally we say *go to the* + noun for place, but in the case of *go to school, go to work, go to bed* and *go home*, the article isn't used. Also point out that we usually say *Everyone's asleep* not *Everyone's sleeping*.
- In pairs, across the class, students ask and answer about people in the different parts of the world.

6 Writing *What's happening?*

- Once again, make it clear to students that in this exercise they aren't writing about normal routines or habits, but about things happening right now. Starting with the time and date should help to locate the events in the immediate present.
- Brainstorm ideas before students start to write.

> **Example answer**
> I'm sitting at my desk and I'm doing an English exercise. My friend Marketa is sitting next to me and we're writing sentences. Our teacher is walking around the room. Outside the window, someone is walking to the canteen and some students are playing volleyball.

Grammar:

Present continuous: negative; questions and short answers

Object pronouns

Communicative tasks:

Talking about present actions

Playing a guessing game

1 Presentation *Are you listening?*

a ● Focus on the photo and ask students to say what's happening here. Elicit the meaning of *chemistry test*.

b ● Ask students to read the three sentences (a–c). Remind them of the noun *dream* in *The Silent Powers*, and point out that here the word is used as a verb.

  ● 📻 Play the recording while students follow in their books and decide which sentence is correct.

  ● Elicit or explain the meaning of new vocabulary: *towards, fans, shout, Come on!*

  ● Drill some of the verb phrases using the negative form of the present continuous.

Answer c

c ● Remind students that these questions, without question words at the beginning, are asking for *Yes* or *No* replies.

  ● Students complete the matching task. Check they are aware of the full forms of *isn't* and *aren't*.

  ● Choose pairs of students to ask and answer the questions across the class.

  ● You can add some other present continuous questions, for example: *Are the other students writing?* (*Yes, they are.*) *Is Joe thinking about chemistry?* (*No, he isn't.*) *Is the teacher talking to Joe?* (*Yes, she is.*)

Answers

1 d 2 c 3 b 4 a

2 Key grammar *Present continuous: negative; questions and short answers*

  ● Students complete the table orally or/and in writing.

Answers

Negative:	isn't
	aren't
Questions:	Is
	Are
Answers:	am
	is; isn't
	aren't

3 Practice

a ● Students complete the paragraph orally and/or in writing, using the present continuous form of the verbs in brackets.

Answers

2 are doing 3 isn't listening 4 is saying

5 aren't listening 6 Are (you) dreaming

b ● Make sure students understand that they have to write negative sentences in the present continuous. The sentences can be true or false.

  ● Encourage them to use a variety of subjects, not only *I*. For example: *We aren't playing tennis. Mr Foster isn't standing near the board. Carlo and Magda aren't watching TV.* You could write up some examples of verbs that they can use (*play, sleep, go home* etc.).

  📻 Pattern drill: TRP, page 14, (Unit 9, Step 2, Drill 1).

4 Speaking

  ● Drill the example with the class. You could demonstrate further by miming an action yourself and asking the class to guess what you're doing. Make sure you continue doing the action until they have guessed correctly.

  ● Invite students to mime actions for the class to guess. If they run out of ideas, you could suggest some of these: *riding a bike, tidying my room, cleaning my teeth, drawing a picture, eating an apple, using a mobile phone, making a sandwich, having a shower.*

Try this!

The last letter of each word has been moved on to the beginning of the following word.

Answer: Joe and his friends are doing a chemistry test.

5 Key pronunciation /ɪŋ/

  ● Ask students to read the words of the rhythm drill before they listen. Explain or elicit the meaning of any new words. You may want to introduce the word *nightmare* (= horrible dream) here.

  ● 📻 Play the recording. Students listen and follow in their books.

  ● 📻 Play the recording again, say the lines aloud and encourage the students to join in. Beat time or click your fingers to emphasise the rhythm.

  ● 📻 Play the recording a third time, pausing after each of the present continuous sentences. Drill the pronunciation, paying particular attention to the *-ing* sound.

  ● You could divide the class in half, with one group reading A's part and the other reading B's.

6 Presentation *Everybody loves me!*

a
- Read out the instruction. Give students a few moments to look at the pictures. Make it clear that these are images from Joe's dream.
- 📻 Play the recording while students listen and follow in their books. Explain the meaning of *waving* and *smiling*, and drill the pronunciation of *photographer* /fə'tɒɡrəfə/.
- Students refer to the text and put the pictures in the right order for the story.
- Draw attention to the pronouns in bold and ask students to say who/what they each refer to in the text.

> **Answers**
>
> Correct order: c, e, b, f, a, d

b
- Ask students to say what is happening in each picture. If they are confident with the vocabulary, you could ask them to cover the text and try to remember the words without looking at them.

7 Key grammar *Object pronouns*

- Write the sentence *He can't see her* on the board. Make it clear that *He* and *her* are both pronouns. *He* is the subject of the verb and *her* is the object.
- Students copy and complete the table.
- Elicit some other example sentences using object pronouns.

> **Answers**
>
> you – you;   he – him;   she – her;
> it – it;   we – us;   they – them

8 Practice

- Tell students to look carefully at the underlined words to decide on the correct pronouns.

📻 Pattern drill: TRP, page 14, (Unit 9, Step 2, Drill 2).

> **Answers**
>
> 2 her   3 me   4 it   5 them
> 6 him   7 you   8 us

9 Speaking *A guessing game*

- You can play this game with the whole class or put students into small groups.
- Demonstrate by giving one or two clues yourself for the class to guess. For example: *I'm walking on it.* (The floor.) *Julia is sitting behind them.* (Miguel and Sandro.)
- For extra help, you could supply some more verbs which the students can use (*talk to, listen to, sit on / behind / in front of* etc.).

> Vocabulary: Clothes
> Communicative tasks:
>   Describing what you're wearing
>   Talking about what you usually wear

1 Key vocabulary *Clothes*

- Focus on the pictures and ask students which words they know in English. Many are likely to be familiar to them, and others may be similar to words in their own language.
- Set a time limit of three minutes. Students read the words and look around for examples of the items in the classroom.
- 📻 Play the recording. Students listen and repeat.
- Ask students to find all the words that are in the plural form. Emphasise that the following are <u>always</u> plural: *jeans, trousers, shorts, (sun)glasses* – they are one garment but with two legs or two lenses. Contrast these with *socks, shoes, trainers, gloves*, etc., which are separate items. We can talk about *a sock* or *one shoe*, but we can't say *a trouser*. You may want to bring in the use of *a pair of* for all these plural words.

2 Listening *Outside the stadium*

a
- Read out the introduction to the listening. Explain that Exeter City and Bristol Rovers are English football clubs and that red white and black are Exeter City's team colours.
- Ask students what they can see in the pictures. Teach or elicit the new words *stadium* and *queue*. Pay particular attention to the pronunciation of *queue* /kjuː/.
- 📻 Read out the question and ask students to listen for the answer. Play the recording.

> **Answer**   Lisa's got the tickets.

Tapescript

JACK: Where is she, Ben? I can't see her.

BEN: Well, we must find her. She's got our tickets in her bag.

JACK: I'm sure she's in the queue somewhere.

BEN: Yes, I know, but it's a very long queue, Jack.

JACK: She's wearing a red, white and black scarf.

BEN: That's not very helpful, Jack. I mean, a lot of people are wearing red, white and black scarves!

JACK: She's got her big, white bear with her. Can you see any bears?

BEN: No, I can't.

JACK: Wait a minute! I can see her. She's wearing her Exeter City hat. She always wears that hat at football matches. Lisa!

BEN: Hang on a minute, Jack! Wait for me!

b ● Choose students to read the questions and explain or elicit the meaning of *carry*.

● 🔊 Play the recording again, twice if necessary. Students listen and then write answers to the questions, in full sentences.

● Draw attention to the difference in tense between the first two questions and the last two, and ask why they are different. Establish that 1 and 2 are asking about what Lisa is wearing <u>at the moment</u>, while, 4 and 5 are asking about her normal habits. (Note that the difference between the two tenses is given more focus in the Module 5 review.)

> **Answers**
> 1 She's wearing a scarf and a hat.
> 2 She's carrying a bear.
> 3 It's an Exeter City hat.
> 4 No, she doesn't.
> 5 She wears it at football matches.

3 Writing and speaking

a ● Read out the examples.

b ● Set a time limit of four minutes. Encourage students to use a mixture of present simple and present continuous verbs, as in the examples. Remind them of other frequency adverbs that may be useful (*always, often, usually*).

● Ask different students to read one or two of their sentences to the class.

4 Speaking *An observation test!*

● Choose two students to read the example dialogue.

● You could go to the back of the classroom, so that the class can't see you, and ask: *What am I wearing?* Invite students to describe your clothes, and correct or confirm their statements as in the dialogue.

● In pairs, students sit back to back and take it in turns to describe each other's clothes.

OPTION

For extra practice of the present continuous, choose a photo of a situation from an earlier unit in the Student's Book and use it as the basis for the 'Picture memory game' (see page 103 in the Teacher's Book). You could award a bonus point for every sentence where the present continuous tense is used correctly.

CHAPTER 7 The Silent Powers
Pictures in the water

OPTION

You could remind students of the story so far by drawing a simple plan on the board. Ask them to identify the places (Seth's cottage, Mr Neil's cottage, the Circle of Seven and Devil's Bridge) and to help you reconstruct the events that happened at each one.

● If you haven't taken up the option above, ask students to say what happened in Chapter 6 of the story. (They can use the present tense for this.)

● 🔊 Refer to the picture and ask *Where is Sophie? Whose faces can Sophie see? What's the name of the dog?* Play the recording (or read the text out if you prefer).

● Ask students to read the text again themselves and to make a note of the words they don't know.

● Ask them to discuss the words in pairs and to try to work out their meaning from the context and by referring to the pictures.

● Go through the events, and elicit or explain the meaning of the new vocabulary.

● Ask these comprehension questions and elicit answers from the class. Alternatively, you could write them on the board and ask students to write down the answers.

1 *Why does Sophie want to go home to London? (Because she's scared.)*

2 *What can Sophie see in the water? (A hill and a cave, the White Lady and the Red Queen.)*

3 *Is the Red Queen destroying the Silent Powers? (No – but she's trying to destroy them.)*

4 *The White Lady says: We're with you all the time. Who are 'we'? (The White Lady, Mr Neil and Cabal.)*

5 *Does the Red Queen know that Sophie wants to go home? (Yes, she does.)*

6 *Is the Red Queen trying to help Sophie? (No, she isn't.)*

7 *Is Cabal attacking Sophie, or is he helping her? (He's helping her.)*

8 *Cabal is with Sophie at the right moment. What mustn't Sophie do? (She mustn't look into the Red Queen's eyes.)*

- 📻 To conclude, play the recording while students follow the story in their books. Ask students why the Red Queen wants Sophie to lose her strength and give up. Have they got any ideas about what Sophie's mission is? Are there any clues in the chapter about the next place she has to go? Discuss these questions in the students' language.

Puzzle task

- Students work individually to discover the missing letter in each pair of words – these letters form the word represented by the rune.
- Ask them to use a dictionary to find out what the word means, if they don't know.

> **Answer** Mystery.

Extra exercises

1
- Point out that a subject pronoun comes before the verb and an object pronoun comes after it.

> **Answers**
> 1 him   2 it   3 me   4 them   5 us   6 it   7 her

2
> **Answers**
> 1 c   2 b   3 b   4 a   5 b

3
- Remind students of the word order for present continuous questions:
  (question word +) be + subject + ...ing.

> **Answers**
> 1   What are you doing?
> 2   Are you eating my crisps?
> 3   Where's Sadie sitting?
> 4   What's Mr Kelly wearing?
> 5   Where's Joe going?
> 6   How many people are watching the match?

4
- Students match the answers with the questions in Exercise 3.

> **Answers**
> 1 f   2 a   3 d   4 e   5 b   6 c

5
> **Answers**
> 1 a   2 b   3 c   4 b   5 c

6
- If students have difficulty remembering any of these words, tell them to use a dictionary or to look back through the unit.

- When you check their answers, ask them to give reasons for their choices.

> **Answers**
> 1 ice cream   2 him   3 rug   4 stairs   5 dreaming

7
- Ask students to work on the translations in pairs or small groups, and then discuss with the whole class.

Extra reading

Sports fans

Lead in

- Ask students about their favourite sports. Help with vocabulary as necessary and write the names of the sports on the board.
- Focus on the photos and establish the names of the sports. Discuss the popularity of these sports in the students' country.

Task

- Ask students to read the texts and to make a note of the words they don't know.
- Ask them to discuss the words in pairs and to try to work out their meaning from the context.
- Check the meaning of the new vocabulary with the students. Point out that *queue* can be used as a verb as well as a noun.
- Students refer back to the texts to decide if the sentences 1–8 are true or false. Ask them to correct the false sentences.
- Draw attention to the use of the present simple in these texts. Establish that the speakers are using this tense because they are talking about things that happen normally or regularly. Ask students to find frequency adverbs and other time expressions that go with the present simple (*usually, sometimes, often, Every year, in June, always*).
- You can ask some further comprehension questions, for example:

  Football: *What does his son collect? (Autographs of his favourite players.) Which team do they support? (Manchester United.)*

  Cricket: *What does the speaker do on holiday? (He watches England when they play cricket.)*

  Tennis: *Why do people wait in a queue at Wimbledon? (To buy tickets.)*

  Motor racing: *When does the British Grand Prix take place? (In July.)*

Answers

1 False. (They're usually on Saturday afternoon.)
2 True.
3 True.
4 True.
5 False. (It takes place in the summer.)
6 True.
7 False. (It's a car race.)
8 False. (It's the name of a place.)

OPTION

Depending on which of the sports students are interested in, you could introduce some associated words, for example:

batsman, racket, goalkeeper, circuit, bat, stadium, net, driver, striker, court, defender, pitch, racing car, bowler, boots.

Ask students to sort them into the categories *People, Places* and *Equipment,* and to write *F* (football), *C* (cricket), *T* (tennis) or *MR* (motor racing) beside each one.

Ask students to come and write them up on the board in the correct category:

People: batsman (C), goalkeeper (F), driver (MR), striker (F), defender (F), bowler (C)

Places: circuit (MR), stadium (F), court (T), pitch (C)

Equipment: racket (T), bat (C), net (T), racing car (MR), boots (F)

10 Plans

Grammar:
Present continuous used for the future
Language for making suggestions
Vocabulary: Future time expressions
Communicative tasks:
Talking about future arrangements
Making and replying to suggestions

1 Key vocabulary *Time expressions*

a ● Focus on the time line and make sure that students understand the meaning of *future*. Explain that *next Tuesday* means 'the Tuesday after today'.

● Ask students to look through the list and find two more expressions that refer to the present (*at the moment, now*). They then copy the time line and write the other expressions on the line in chronological order.

● 🔊 Play the recording for students to check their answers and repeat.

● You may want to point out that *this evening* and *tonight* can be present time expressions as well as future ones, depending on the time of speaking (for example, *They aren't at home – they're having dinner at a restaurant this evening / tonight.*).

Tapescript/Answers

Present (in any order):
1–3 today, at the moment, now
Future:
4 this evening   7 at the weekend
5 tonight   8 next week
6 tomorrow   9 next month

OPTION

You could introduce a few more time expressions: *this afternoon, tomorrow morning/afternoon/ evening/night, next summer/winter*. Ask students to write them on the line. Draw attention to the use of *tomorrow*, not *next*, when we are talking about the day after today (*tomorrow morning*, NOT *next morning*).

b ● Students complete the sentences, orally and/or in writing, with the correct information.

Answers
1–3 [students' own answers]   4 At the weekend
5 At the moment

2 Presentation *Making arrangements*

a ● Choose students to read out the email messages. Elicit or explain the meaning of *dentist* and *busy* and establish that all the messages are referring to the future.

● In pairs, students match the invitations/suggestions with the replies.

● 🔊 Play the recording. Students listen and check their answers.

● 🔊 Focus on the different ways of making invitations and suggestions: *Can you ...? / Let's ... / Why don't we ...? / Shall we ...?* and on the replies: *Yes, I can. / Yes, that's fine. / Sorry, but I can't.* Play the recording again, pausing after these expressions and asking students to repeat.

● You could ask students to practise reading the messages and replies in pairs.

Answers
Number 3 goes with number 2.
Number 6 goes with number 4.

b ● Draw attention to the use of the present continuous in the email messages. Ask: *Are these things happening now? (No – they're in the future.)*.

● Establish that the events (the guitar lesson, the dentist, the party) are already arranged.

● Students ask and answer the questions.

Answers
1   She's having a party.
2   Yes, he is.
3   No, he isn't. (He's going to the dentist.)
4   Yes, she is. (She's having a guitar lesson.)
5   At 10.30.
6   Outside the sports centre.

3 Key grammar
Present continuous used for the future

● Draw attention to the future time expressions. Emphasise again that in these sentences the present continuous doesn't refer to the present but to definite arrangements in the future.

Answer   Column C.

4 Practice

a ● Students write each sentence with the correct verb in the present continuous.

> **Answers**
> 2 We're meeting Danny at seven o'clock.
> 3 I'm going to the dentist tomorrow.
> 4 We're having an English test on Friday.
> 5 Tom's watching a video with Rick this evening.

b ● Focus on the examples and make sure that the task is clear. Elicit one or two more examples of each type of sentence.

   ● Give students a few minutes to write their sentences before they test each other in pairs.

   🎧 Pattern drill: TRP, page 14, (Unit 10, Step 1).

5 Speaking

a ● Say the dialogue line by line and ask students to repeat. Pay attention to the intonation and stress.

b ● Students practise the dialogue in pairs.

   ● They then substitute other times and activities. Encourage them to think of other activities as well as the ones in the list.

> **Try this!**
> Answers: Saturday, December, Monday, Sunday, February, October, Wednesday, Friday, January, Tuesday, September, Thursday, November

6 Key grammar *Suggestions*

● Make it clear that the three expressions for making suggestions mean much the same in English, although *Let's …* is a stronger expression of preference than the other two.

● Discuss the translations with the class.

● Elicit appropriate replies for each example, using *Yes, that's fine* or *Sorry, but I can't.*

● Starting with the first example, you can prompt students with other words to substitute. For example:

Saturday	(*Let's play on Saturday.*)
meet	(*Let's meet on Saturday.*)
Why don't we …?	(*Why don't we meet on Saturday?*)
go shopping	(*Why don't we go shopping on Saturday?*)
Shall we	(*Shall we go shopping on Saturday?*)
play tennis	(*Shall we play tennis on Saturday?*)
tomorrow	(*Shall we play tennis tomorrow?*)

7 Practice

● Students read the dialogue and put the sentences in the right places, orally and/or in writing.

● Check the answers by asking a pair of students to read out the completed dialogue. Students work in pairs and practise the dialogue.

> **Answers**
> 1 Why don't we go bowling?
> 2 Let's stay at home.
> 3 Shall we watch TV?
> 4 Let's look.

OPTION

For further practice, refer students to Tom's email message in 2a and ask them to write a reply.
For example:
Hi Tom,
Yes, that's fine. Let's play on Saturday afternoon.
Shall we meet at the park at 2.30?
Rick

8 Speaking

● Go through list A and make sure that students are familiar with all the adjectives.

● In pairs, students take it in turns to read out a sentence and to reply with a suggestion.

● Choose students to say their matching sentences. Elicit other possible suggestions from the class, for example:

   1 *Shall we sit down?*
   2 *Why don't we watch a video?*
   3 *Let's go swimming.*
   4 *Shall we buy a pizza?*
   5 *Let's have some orange juice.*

> **Answers**
> 1 c 2 a 3 e 4 b 5 d

9 Writing *Messages*

● Students exchange messages making suggestions.

> **Example answers**
> Hi Clare
> What are you doing on Sunday morning?
> Why don't we go to the beach?
> Jane
>
> Hi Jane
> Yes, that's fine. Let's meet at the bus station at 10 o'clock.
> Clare

Grammar: Future with *going to*

Communicative tasks:

    Talking about plans and intentions

    Making a notice of 'good intentions'

1 Presentation *What are you going to do?*

BACKGROUND

The Natural History Museum in South Kensington first opened in 1881 and it now holds a collection of over 70 million plants, animals, fossils, rocks and minerals from around the world. The exhibitions are divided into two areas: the Life Galleries (about life on Earth) and the Earth Galleries (about the evolution of our planet). Many of the exhibits are displayed with interactive video technology that allows people to take an active part in discovering and 'experiencing' the workings of the natural world. Behind the scenes, more than 350 scientists are engaged in research on the museum's huge collections. Up to 1,200 school pupils visit the museum every weekday. Admission is free.

a
- Focus on the photos and ask students to name the people they know and to identify the teacher. Ask: *Where are they?* (*At a museum.*).
- Elicit or explain the meaning of *dinosaur, whale* and *fossil,* and ask students to find these things in the photos. Invite suggestions about what else we can see at a natural history museum.

> **Answers**
>
> a fossil b whale c dinosaur

b
- Read out the introduction to the dialogue. Make it clear that the class is in the entrance hall of the museum. You might want to introduce the word *gallery* at this point.
- 🎙 Read out the instruction and the question. With books closed, students listen and answer. Emphasise that Jack and his friends are talking about their plans for their museum visit.

> **Answer** The beginning.

c
- 🎙 Play the recording again while students listen and follow in their books.
- Read out the questions and elicit the full form of *Who's* (*Who is*). Students write the names of the people.
- 🎙 Play the recording once again. Pause after the questions and answers with *going to* and ask the students to repeat.
- You may also want to drill some of the useful expressions in the dialogue (*That's a good idea. That's nice. Listen, everyone!*).

> **Answers**
>
> 1 Lisa 2 Jack 3 Mr White
> 4 Sadie and Lisa 5 Ben

2 Key grammar *going to*

- Emphasise that *going to* + infinitive is used for definite plans for the future – the people in the dialogue know exactly what they're going to do at the museum.
- Look at the affirmative and negative examples and elicit the full forms of the verb *be*.
- Students complete the examples orally and/or in writing.

> **Answers**
>
> Is
> Are
> are
> 'm not; isn't

3 Practice

a
- Students put the words in the right order to make sentences.

> **Answers**
>
> 1 We're going to take some photos.
> 2 He isn't going to draw a fossil.
> 3 They're going to look at the dinosaurs.
> 4 Are you going to see the blue whale?
> 5 I'm going to have a cup of tea.

b
- In pairs, students talk about plans for a visit to the museum, using *going to*. They can adapt the sentences from the dialogue in 1b or they can add other ideas, following their own interests.

OPTION

For further practice using the dialogue, say some sentences which are false and ask students to correct them. For example:

– *Jack's going to take photos of the dinosaur. (No, he isn't. He's going to draw the dinosaur.)*

– *Ben's going to visit Gallery 11. (No, he isn't. He's going to visit Gallery 31.)*

– *Sadie and Lisa are going to look at fossils. (No, they aren't. They're going to look at the blue whale.)*

– *They're going to meet at two o'clock. (No, they aren't. They're going to meet at one o'clock.)*

4 Reading and speaking
A dinosaur, please.

a • Read through the lists with the class and make sure that everyone is familiar with all the words. Make it clear that the animals you can buy at the museum shop are plastic models.

b • Students plan their purchases. Remind them that they have only have a total of £10 to spend. Explain what the equivalent value would be in their currency.
 • Ask different students to tell the class how they are going to spend their money.

🔊 Pattern drill: TRP, page 14, (Unit 10, Step 2).

5 Listening *Song*

 • 🔊 Play the song through and allow students to enjoy listening to it, with books closed. Ask them to say any words or phrases they heard.
 • Ask students to read the two lists of words and to predict the way they match.
 • 🔊 Play the song again. Students listen for the words in the lists and then make sentences with *going to*. They could work on this in pairs.
 • Point out the use of the present continuous in *I'm leaving tonight.* Explain that the meaning is very similar to *I'm going to leave tonight*, but it's expressing a definite arrangement. The other sentences with *going to* are saying what he plans or intends to do.
 • 🔊 Ask students to turn to the song words on page 144. Play the song once again and encourage them to join in.

Answers
I'm going to catch a train.
I'm going to find a better place.
I'm going to leave this job.
I'm going to be free.

6 Key pronunciation /ə/

 • Ask students to read the sentences to themselves and notice where the main stress falls.
 • 🔊 Students listen and repeat. Use your hand to beat out the strong stresses and draw attention to the /ə/ sound in the unstressed *to*. Drill the stressed words in isolation and then again in complete sentences,

7 Writing *My resolutions*

 • Explain the meaning of *resolutions* and *good intentions* and choose students to read out the examples from the school magazine.
 • Students write similar resolutions with *(not) going to*. Display their work in the classroom if possible.

Example answer
I'm not going to be late with my homework.
I'm going to be more polite.
I'm going to tidy my room every week.

Vocabulary: The weather
Communicative tasks:
 Talking about the weather
 Writing a holiday postcard

1 Reading *A postcard from Mel*

BACKGROUND

There are three terms in the British school year. with a **half term** break in each and a long holiday from late July to early September. The summer half term is usually a week from late May to early June.

Cordoba's **Mezquita** or Great Mosque, built in the 10th–11th centuries by the city's Moorish rulers, is one of the world's great buildings with striped arches supported by a forest of magnificent pillars. The mosque was taken over as a place of Christian worship in the 13th century and a cathedral was set up in the middle of it in the 17th century – but the splendour of the original design still remains.

a • Look at the photo and ask: *Who's this? (Mel.) What's she doing? (She's writing a postcard.)*
 • Read out the introductory sentence and explain the words *half term* and *pen friend*.
 • Students read Mel's postcard to answer the question.
 • Ask students to use the picture of Mel to guess the meaning of *balcony*, and to work out the meaning of *market* from its context.

Answer She's in Cordoba, in Spain.

b • Read out the questions and set a time limit of two minutes for students to write the answers.
 • Ask students to identify the tenses of the verbs in Mel's postcard and to say whether they're referring to the past or the future.

Answers
1 She's sitting on the balcony at Rosa's flat.
2 She's visiting the Mezquita.
3 Yes – they're going to the market.
4 She's going to buy a bag.

2 Key vocabulary *The weather*

- 🔊 Introduce the word *weather* and then play the recording. Students listen, and repeat the words.
- If you wish, test comprehension by asking students to translate the weather words into their language.
- Choose students to ask and answer about today's weather across the class.

1 To practise more of the vocabulary, you could mime being in different weather conditions, or invite students to do so. The class has to guess what the weather is like.

2 You may want to add other words to the list, for example: *It's fine/warm/cool/freezing/stormy/humid.*

3 You could ask students to record the vocabulary by illustrating the words themselves. For example:

3 Writing *A holiday postcard*

- This exercise can be done in class or set for homework.

Example answer

Dear Richard,

At the moment I'm sitting outside with Dad at a café in Rome and we're eating ice cream. It's sunny here today, but it isn't very hot. This evening we're going to a concert with some friends and tomorrow we're visiting the Forum. This is a fabulous city!

See you soon.

Love, Sonia

CHAPTER 8 The Silent Powers
The meeting

- Ask some questions to revise the previous chapter.
  - *Who said this to Sophie: 'Now she knows you're strong'? (The White Lady.) Who is 'she'? (The Red Queen.)*
  - *Who said this to Sophie: 'Give me the moonstone ... you can go home and be happy again'? (The Red Queen.) Where is 'home'? (London.)*
  - *Who helped Sophie to escape? (Cabal.)*

- Tell students that now it's the next day. Ask: *What must Sophie do today?* (*She must meet the White Lady and bring Epona.*)
- Look at the picture with the class. Ask students to name the people and animals and to say where they are.
- 🔊 Play the recording (or read the chapter out if you prefer) and help with key vocabulary (*king, gate, ring, nervous, What's the matter?, call, Good luck!*).
- Ask these comprehension questions and elicit answers from the class. Alternatively, you could write them on the board and ask students to write down the answers.

  1 *What is Sophie going to do this morning? (She's going to go riding / to meet the White Lady.)*
  2 *Why can't she go this afternoon? (Because a friend is phoning her from New York.)*
  3 *Where is Cabal taking Sophie and Epona? (To the Circle of Seven.)*
  4 *Who is waiting for them with the White Lady? (Mr Neil.)*
  5 *What is Sophie's last test? (She must find King's Hill and open the Gate of Rings.)*
  6 *Is the White Lady going to go with Sophie? (No, she isn't.)*
  7 *Why can the text message help Sophie? (Because it's a map.)*
  8 *Why is Epona nervous? (Because the king is calling her.)*

- 🔊 Play the recording once more while students follow the story in their books. Ask students to look back at the text message in Chapter 1 (page 33). Do they have any ideas about how this works as a map? What do they think Sophie is going to find at King's Hill? What could Mr Neil mean when he says that the king is calling Epona? Discuss these questions in the students' language.
- Choose students to read out the dialogue between Sophie and Mr Neil.
- Ask students to practise reading the dialogue at the Circle of Seven in pairs.
- Invite one or two pairs to act out the scene for the class.

Puzzle task

- Students work individually to discover the coded word. (The numbers refer to the position of the letters in the alphabet, working backwards – so Z = 1, Y = 2, etc.)

Answer team

Extra exercises

1
- As you check the answers, elicit some example sentences using the alternative answers in questions 1 and 2 (for example, *I'm going to France in July / I'm going home at 4.30. Let's stop ... / Why don't we stop ...?*)

Answers

1 b 2 b 3 c 4 c 5 a

2 ● You can ask students to cover the alternatives below the text and to predict what the missing words will be as they read. They then look at the alternatives and choose the correct answers.

Answers

1 a 2 c 3 b 4 c 5 b

3 ● Remind students to look at the time expressions to help them decide whether the verbs have a present or a future meaning.

Answers

1 Future 2 Present 3 Present 4 Future
5 Future 6 Present

4 ● Tell students that they need to look carefully at Tom's answers to work out what the questions should be.

● You could do the first one together with the class. Emphasise the use of *next week*, telling us that the question is referring to the future. Point out that Tom's answer isn't *Yes* or *No*, so we need a question word at the beginning of the question.

● Students may suggest a question with *going to* instead of the present continuous: *Where are you going to go?* Let them know that this is quite correct – the distinction between *going to* for plans and the present continuous for arrangements is often a fine one, and the two forms can be almost interchangeable. The same applies to other questions in this dialogue: Gill could ask: (2) *Are you going to walk there?* and (3) *What are you doing there?* – these questions are not incorrect, although they don't completely match the answers that Jack gives.

Example answers

1 Where are you going
2 Are you going
3 What are you going to do/see
4 Are you going to see / look at
5 going to buy

5 ## Answers

1 c 2 c 3 b 4 b 5 b

6 ● Ask students to work on the translations in pairs or small groups, and then discuss with the whole class.

Extra reading

An exchange visit

BACKGROUND

Some schools in the USA have half- or full-year exchange programmes designed to give foreign students first-hand experience of a different culture and a different educational system. Students are housed by host families who usually have children attending the host school.

Lead in

● Ask students about their contacts in other countries (they may have family members as well as friends living abroad) and about the places they want to visit in the future.

Task

● Explain the meaning of *school exchange*. Refer to the map and ask: *Where does Donna usually go to school? (In Scotland.) Where is she going to school at the moment? (In the USA.)*

● Focus on the photos and ask students to say what they can about Donna's life in Kansas.

● Ask students to read the text themselves, and to try to guess the meaning of new words from their context and from the photos. Point out that they don't need to know every single word to grasp the meaning of the text.

● Elicit or explain the meaning of any new vocabulary (*choir, host family, ranch* etc.).

● Choose students to read out the questions. Tell the class to look carefully at the question words to make sure they're giving the correct information.

● Students refer back to the text to answer the questions. Ask them to write in full sentences. Check answers.

● Pick out some of the present continuous verbs in the text and ask if they refer to the present or the future. (They refer to the future.) Ask students to find some verbs in the present simple and ask why this tense is used. Make sure they recognise that Donna uses the present simple to describe things that happen regularly or all the time.

Answers

1 Her home is in Glasgow, Scotland.
2 She plays basketball.
3 It meets on Wednesday afternoon.
4 They talk about their life in Kansas.
5 She's staying on a ranch in Kansas.
6 She's going to New York next week.
7 She's going to visit the Empire State Building and lots of other places.

Module 5 Review

Language summary

1 Present continuous

1.1 ● Students make full sentences using the present continuous.

Answers

2 Our teacher is/isn't using a computer at the moment.
3 I'm (not) sitting near the window today.
4 We aren't having our lunch at the moment.
5 It is/isn't raining at the moment.
6 I'm doing an English exercise.

1.2 ● Students make present continuous questions to fit with the answers. They may think of slightly different questions from the ones below.

Example answers

2 What are you writing?
3 Where are you going?
4 What are you reading/writing?
5 What are you watching?

2 Present continuous + future time expressions

● After checking that students have the right prepositions, you can put them in pairs to ask and answer the questions.

Answers

2 on 3 at 4 in 5 at 6 on

2 When are Monsoon playing at your/our school?
    On Friday.
3 When are you going home?
    At four o'clock.
4 When are Sadie's cousins coming to England?
    In August.
5 When's Mel going swimming?
    At the weekend.
6 When are we having a maths test?
    On Monday.

3 The future with *going to*

● Students should write down their guesses for what the people are going to do. Then choose students to ask and answer across the class.

Example answers

2 What's Rick going to do?
    He's going to watch TV.
3 What's Danny going to do?
    He's going to visit a friend.
4 What's Tom going to do?
    He's going to go to the supermarket.
5 What's Kim going to do?
    She's going to write a letter.

4 Object pronouns

● Tell students to write object pronouns that agree with the underlined words.

Answers

2 him 3 it 4 us 5 me
6 them 7 her 8 you

5 Making suggestions

● Remind students that the three expressions have almost the same meaning. There are lots of different alternatives that they could think of for these responses.

Example answers

2 Shall we have a drink?
3 Let's go to the cinema tomorrow.
4 Why don't we play a computer game?
5 Let's play football.
6 Shall we get some tickets for the concert on Friday?

6 Present continuous or present simple?

● Ask students to make other sentences to show the difference between the two tenses.

Answers

1 go 2 's/is going 3 'm/am eating
4 's/is snowing 5 gets up 6 doesn't like

Study skills 5　Parts of speech

- Look at the example sentence with the class and discuss the function of each part of speech.
- Write the example sentence on the board. Ask students to come up and substitute alternative words in the sentence. For example:

  Her brother thinks she is brilliant!

  My teacher thinks I am lazy!

- Ask students to play the memory game in pairs. Provide each pair with paper and ask them to cut it into 24 slips. They then work together to write eight words in each category. They can go on to play the game with their own words, or you could ask them to exchange words with another pair.
- In their pairs, students lay the words face down on the desk and mix them up. They then take it in turns to turn over two words. If they are the same part of speech, they take the words and have another turn. If the words don't match, they replace them in their positions face down on the desk, and the other partner takes a turn. The person with the most words at the end of the game is the winner. Monitor as many of the students as possible. Weaker students may need extra help.
- Remind students of the dictionary abbreviations for these parts of speech. Point out that some words can be used as different parts of speech (for example, *queue* – noun and verb; *clean* – verb and adjective).

OPTION

Write these patterns on the board and elicit sentences to fit, for example:

1　*Pronoun – verb – noun. (They play football.)*

2　*Possessive adjective – noun – verb – noun. (Our cat eats fish.)*

3　*Pronoun – verb – possessive adjective – adjective – noun. (I like your new trainers.)*

4　*Possessive adjective – adjective – noun – verb – preposition – the – noun. (His Australian friends are sitting on the beach.)*

How's it going?

Your rating

- Students look back at the exercises in the Language summary and make their own assessment of how well they understand and remember the material.

Vocabulary

- Students test their memory of the words they have learnt in two of the vocabulary categories.
- You could follow up with a game of 'Word tennis' (see page 103 in the Teacher's Book).

Test a friend

- Look at the example questions and elicit the correct answers.
- Students refer back to the texts in Units 9 and 10 and write questions about them to test their partner. They then ask and answer in pairs.

Write to your teacher

- Use the students' letters to find out what they are enjoying and where they are having difficulties. Reply to the letters with a personal message in the students' language, giving help, praise and encouragement.

Your Workbook

- Students should complete the Learning diary when they come to the end of each unit.

Coursework　All about me!

My clothes

Students write about:
- the clothes they wear
- clothes they like and dislike

- Focus on the photos. Ask students to say where Jack is and to describe the clothes that he's wearing.
- Ask students to read the text and make a note of any new vocabulary. Elicit or explain new words (*hate, comfortable, expensive* etc.). Point out that Jack describes the things he wears at school and in his free time, and that he expresses his own opinions about certain types of clothes.
- Draw attention to the use of different tenses. Mostly Jack uses the present simple because he's talking about his normal habits and preferences. However, in the first sentence (about his school uniform) he uses the present continuous because he's talking about this particular photo.
- Invite students to discuss the clothes they like and dislike and the different places where they buy their clothes. Encourage a range of different views, for example, ask if students think it is more important that clothes are comfortable or fashionable? Make sure no one is made to feel uncomfortable if they don't spend a lot of money on clothes.
- Ask students to plan their text. They should write three or four paragraphs and illustrate them as they wish.
- Set a time limit, allowing one or two weeks for work on the project. If students want to spend longer on this work, you could negotiate an extension of time. The work should be mainly done at home.
- Ask students to check their text before they copy it out and design their page. Tell them to use Jack's text as a model and remind them to look back at Units 9 and 10 if they need help with language.

Module 6

Looking back

See page 7 of the Introduction for ideas on how to use the Module opening pages

11 About the past

STEP 1

Grammar: *was/were*
Vocabulary: Occupations
Communicative tasks:
   Talking about people from the past
   Playing a quiz game about famous people

1 Key vocabulary *Occupations*

- You could start by introducing the word *occupations* (= jobs) and asking students to say any names for occupations that they know in English.
- Read out the words in the list.
- Focus on the pictures. In pairs students try to match the words with the pictures.
- 🔊 Play the recording. Students listen and check their answers and say the words. Draw attention to the use of the indefinite article in these sentences.
- Point out the common form of verb + *-er* or *-or* for names of occupations (other examples: *teacher, dancer, driver, baker, builder, waiter, sailor*). You could introduce *waiter – waitress* as another occupation, like *actor – actress*, where the name has a masculine and a feminine form.

Tapescript/Answers

1	I'm a pop star.	5	They're singers.
2	We're scientists.	6	We're explorers.
3	She's an actress.	7	She's a painter.
4	He's an actor.	8	He's a writer.

2 Presentation *Who were they?*

a
- Refer students to the quiz sentences, but tell them to concentrate only on the names. Set a time limit of three minutes. In pairs, students try to match the names with the photos. If they aren't sure, ask them to guess.
- Check the answers with the class before going on to 2b.

Answers
a William Shakespeare   b Pablo Picasso
c Maria Montessori   d George Washington and Abraham Lincoln   e Christopher Columbus
f Albert Einstein   g Kurt Cobain   h Laika
i Marie Sklodowska-Curie and Pierre Curie
j The Beatles

b
- Introduce the verb *was born* as a fixed phrase (don't go into explanations about the passive form here) and explain the meaning of *space* and *spaceship*.
- Ask students to read the quiz sentences and work in pairs to see if they can find the four mistakes.
- 🔊 Play the recording. Students read the sentences and pick out the four mistakes.
- Point out that all these sentences refer to the past. Draw attention to the /ə/ sound in the unstressed *was* and *were*.

Tapescript/Answers

(As in the Student's Book, except for these:)
1   Pablo Picasso was a painter. He was <u>Spanish</u>.
3   Albert Einstein was a <u>scientist</u>. He was born in Germany.
7   Marie Sklodowska-Curie and Pierre Curie were scientists. Pierre was French, but <u>Marie was born in Poland</u>.
9   George Washington and Abraham Lincoln were American <u>presidents</u>.

c
- 🔊 Students listen to the sentences and decide who is speaking. Check answers. Elicit the full form of *wasn't* (*was not*) and *weren't* (*were not*).
- 🔊 Drill the sentences, using the recording.

Answers
1   Albert Einstein.
2   Marie Sklodowska-Curie
3   Picasso
4   George Washington and Abraham Lincoln

3 Key grammar *was/were*

- Emphasise that *was* and *were* are the past forms of *is* and *are*.
- Ask students to complete the table orally and/or in writing.

Answers
wasn't
were
was
weren't

4 Practice

a • Students fill in the past tense forms orally and/or in writing.

> **Answers**
>
> 1 Was   2 were   3 Were   4 was   5 Was   6 Was

b • Elicit answers to the questions in 4a. Students then ask and answer in pairs.

c • Encourage them to continue with other questions, for example:

Where was Pierre Curie born?

Was Maria Montessori a scientist? (etc.)

🔊 Pattern drill: TRP, page 15, (Unit 11, Step 1).

> **Answers**
>
> 1   Yes, he was.
> 2   They were pop stars.
> 3   Yes, they were.
> 4   He was an explorer.
> 5   No, he wasn't. (He was Italian.)
> 6   Yes, she was.

5 Listening *Ghosts*

a • Focus on the picture and ask students what they can see. Establish that the house is in Paris.

• Remind students of the word *ghost* from Unit 5. Tell them they are going to hear a ghost speaking from the house in the picture.

• 🔊 Play the recording, twice if necessary. Students guess the name of the ghost.

• Point out that the ghost uses the past tense because he's talking about the past, when he was alive.

> **Answer** Pablo Picasso.

Tapescript

WOMAN: Aagh! Who are you?

GHOST: Don't worry. It's all right. I'm a … visitor.

WOMAN: What do you want? Why are you here?

GHOST: This was my house – a long, long time ago.

WOMAN: Oh, I see … Er … Were you born here?

GHOST: No, I wasn't. I wasn't French. I was Spanish. I was born in Malaga in 1881. I wasn't happy at school. But I was very good at art. My father was a painter, you know. I was a painter too. My name was Pablo …

WOMAN: I can't hear you.

GHOST: I'm sorry. I must go. Goodbye …

WOMAN: Wait a minute! Come back! I want to know your name!

b • Ask students to read the questions and to predict the answers.

• 🔊 Play the recording again. Students give their answers in full sentences.

c • In pairs, students ask and answer.

> **Answers**
>
> 2   I was Spanish.
> 3   No, I wasn't.
> 4   Yes, I was.
> 5   No, I wasn't.
> 6   My name was Pablo Picasso.

6 Writing and speaking *Quiz*

• Give students time to write at least two sentences – more if they can. Make it clear that the people they choose should be dead or no longer active in their field, so the sentences must be in the past tense.

• In turn, students read out their questions and invite others to answer. They can do this as a whole class or in groups. If the answer is *False*, ask students to give the correct information if they can.

OPTION

You could make a list of famous people from the past (Cleopatra, Elvis Presley, Beethoven, etc.) and give one name to each student. Allow them a day or so to check up on some basic facts about this person and then ask them to present a short 'ghost's story' using *was* and *were*, like the one in Exercise 5. The other students listen and guess the name of the person.

Grammar: Past simple (affirmative): regular verbs

Communicative tasks:

Talking about events in the past

Writing about an imaginary person's life

STEP 2

1 Reading *Z is for zoo*

a • Give students a few moments to read the definitions in order to choose the answer.

• You could focus on the phonetic transcription of *zoology* and *zoologist*. Take the words syllable by syllable and help students to work out the pronunciation.

> **Answer** c

b • Read out the sentences and explain the new vocabulary: *office*, *forest* and *jungle*.

• Students work with a partner to guess if the sentences are true or false. Check answers with the class.

- Ask if anyone in the class would like to be a zoologist. What qualities does a zoologist need? What are the good points and the difficulties of the job?

2 Presentation *She worked in Africa*

BACKGROUND

Jane Goodall was 26 when, overcoming resistance from the British authorities, she went to live in the Tanzanian jungle to study the wild chimpanzees in 1960. Her patient and careful observation over a period of years produced great discoveries about the animals' behaviour – we now know, for instance, that they hunt, use tools and have distinct personalities. Her work has been carried on by Tanzanian zoologists. Jane Goodall has received many awards for her exceptional contribution to zoology. The Jane Goodall Institute which she set up not only supports further research into chimpanzees but promotes action to improve the environment of all living things.

a
- Ask about the photos and use them to introduce some of the key words from the text: *wild animals, chimpanzees, binoculars.*
- If you have a map, show the location of Tanzania.

b
- 🔊 Play the recording while students listen and follow in their books. Elicit the meaning of *ambition, company, saved (money), travelled* and *accepted.*
- Point out that the first three paragraphs of the text are about finished events in the past, and draw attention to the change in the last paragraph (*Now ...*).
- Focus on the caption under photo 1. Ask students to find suitable captions for the other photos.

Example answers
2 When she was a child she loved animals.
3 She watched from a distance. / She used binoculars.
4 The animals accepted her.

c
- Choose students to read out the sentences. They then refer back to the text to put the events in order (1–8). They could work on this in pairs.
- Check answers with the whole class.
- You can ask some further questions to test comprehension, for example:
  What was Jane's ambition? (To study wild animals in Africa.)
  How did she get money to travel? (She worked with a film company and in a hotel.)

Why was it difficult to get close to the chimpanzees? (Because they were scared of her.)
What did she use to watch the animals? (Binoculars.)
Is she living in Africa now? (No, she isn't.)

Answers
Correct order: 1 b   2 f   3 g   4 e
5 h   6 a   7 d   8 c

3 Key grammar *Past simple: regular verbs*

a
- Look at the examples and remind students that they refer to events in the past.
- Students say the verb ending.

Answer ed

b
- Students copy and complete the table.
- Read out the past simple verbs and ask students to repeat. Note the extra syllable for the *-ed* ending in *wanted.*
- Draw attention to the spelling rules when we add an *-ed* ending (see page 142 in the Student's Book). (Note that in American English the final *l* in words like *travel* is not doubled *travel – traveled*).

Answers
1 lived   2 study   3 loved   4 travelled   5 wanted

4 Practice

a
- Students complete the sentences (orally and/or in writing) with past simple verbs from Exercise 3b.

Answers
2 loved   3 lived/worked/studied   4 travelled
5 worked   6 studied/loved

b
- Look at the example. Refer students back to the text in Exercise 2 and elicit one or two more examples of false sentences which the class can correct. For example:
  When Jane was a child, she loved football. Her favourite book was Harry Potter. *She worked in a shop.*
- Give students time to write at least one false sentence – more if possible. In pairs, they take it in turns to say their sentences and to correct their partner's.

OPTIONS

1 You could turn this activity into a team game. Teams work together to write six false sentences. They then take it in turns to say a sentence and the opposite team gets a point if they can correct the error.

2 Past tense verbs can be used for 'Noughts and crosses' (see page 103). Put infinitives of regular verbs in the grid and ask students to make sentences using the past simple form.

5 Key pronunciation /d/ /t/ /ɪd/

a ● Ask students to read the words of the rhythm drill before they listen. Help with new vocabulary.

● 📻 Play the recording. Students listen and follow in their books.

● 📻 Play the recording again, say the lines aloud and encourage the students to join in. Beat time or click your fingers to emphasise the rhythm.

● 📻 Play the recording a third time, pausing after each line. Drill the subject and verb in isolation and then in the whole line, paying particular attention to the -ed ending.

b ● Say the verbs *picked* and *waited* and ask students to repeat. Make sure they say *picked* as a single syllable /pɪkt/.

● Ask them to say the other verbs and list them according to the sound patterns.

● Point out that normally the -ed ending is pronounced as a /d/ or /t/ sound at the end of the verb. However, verbs that already end in /d/ or /t/ have an extra syllable when we add -ed.

> **Answers**
> 1 stopped, walked   2 wanted, accepted

6 Writing *A famous zoologist*

● Here students use parts of the text in Exercise 2 as a model for a short biography. Make it clear that instead of writing about Jane Goodall and chimpanzees in Africa, they should choose one of the examples listed or think of their own. Elicit or explain the meaning of *tiger* and *penguin*.

● Go through the plan and point out that the first two paragraphs must be in the past simple. Ask students to think of a name for their zoologist and to jot down ideas for their three paragraphs.

● The writing can be completed for homework.

> **Example answer**
> Klaus Braun was born in Berlin in 1968. When he was a child, he loved TV programmes about animals. He wanted to learn about wild animals in India.
>
> He travelled to northern India when he was 28. He lived in the forest and he studied tigers.
>
> Now he is famous and he travels all over the world. He teaches people about Indian tigers and his books are very popular.

> **Try this!**
> Answers: teacher doctor nurse
> actor scientist zoologist

> Vocabulary: Past simple: *Wh-* questions
> Communicative task: Describing childhood

1 Presentation *What did you like?*

a ● Ask students about the photos. Remind them that Ben is Jack's best friend and make it clear that the little boy is Ben when he was a young child. Ask them to say how old they think he was, and why he was nervous.

b ● 📻 Read out the question. Explain *early childhood* and remind students of the meaning of *primary school*. Play the recording while they listen and follow in their books. They answer the question.

● Ask students to find all the past simple verbs in the text and elicit the meaning of *hated*. Say the verbs and ask students to repeat.

● You could ask them to find sentences in the text to describe each of the photos.

> **Answer** No, he wasn't.

c ● Explain the meaning of *at first*.

● Ask students to read the questions and write Ben's answers. Remind them that he is talking about things that happened in the past, so the verbs must be in the past simple.

d ● Check the answers, then students ask and answer the questions across the class.

> **Answers**
> 2 No, I wasn't.
> 3 I liked the books in the library and Sports Day.
> 4 I hated maths.
> 5 I wanted to be a pilot.

2 Key grammar *Past simple:* Wh- *questions*

● Draw attention to the use of *did* in the question form and explain that it is the past simple form of *do*. Compare the use of *do/does* in present simple questions. Point out that the form of *did* remains the same for all subjects.

> **Answer** did

3 Practice

a ● Remind students that Lisa is Sadie's friend. Point out that the sentences are in the past form because they're about her life in the past.

- Students read the answers and write the questions. Tell them to look carefully at the underlined words to work out which question words to use.

> **Answers**
> 2 What did she watch on TV?
> 3 When / What time did school start?
> 4 When / What time did she arrive?
> 5 When / What time did her lessons finish?
> 6 Who did she visit?
> 7 What did she want to be?

b
- In pairs, across the class, students practise asking and answering the questions.
- Contrast this verb form with that of the verb *be*, where we don't use any form of *do* when making questions. Refer to the example in the Remember! box.

🔈 Pattern drill: TRP, page 15, (Unit 1, Step 3).

4 Writing and speaking *Your early childhood*

- Stimulate ideas by asking students a few questions about their childhood, for example: *When did you start school? Were you nervous at first? What were the teachers like? Where did you play after school? What did you like/hate as a child?* You could tell them some memories of your own childhood.
- Ask students to write sentences about their memories. They then make some questions that they would like to ask their partner.
- In pairs, students ask and answer. Ask some students to report on their partner's answers.
- If students happen to misuse some irregular past verb forms here, repeat their sentence with the error corrected but don't go into explanations at this stage.

OPTION

As an extended writing task, students could write a paragraph about themselves and their partner when they were little. For example:
We both started school when we were five, but we were at different schools. I hated school at first, but Julie loved it. She was good at all her subjects. I liked sport and I was interested in …

King's Hill and the Gate of Rings

BACKGROUND

Merlin the wizard can be traced to early Celtic folklore, but he is most commonly associated with the stories of King Arthur. According to legend, Merlin brought up the young Arthur, and his magic helped him to win the crown by pulling the sword Excalibur from the rock in which it was embedded. (For more information on King Arthur, see the note in Unit 12, page 98.)

- Ask students to say what happened in Chapter 8. Ask: *What's Sophie's 'last test' – what must she do?* (*Find King's Hill and open the Gate of Rings.*)
- Focus on the small picture of the hill. Ask students to work out what *T* and *SSS* refer to in the text message. Ask: *Where's Sophie now?* (*At King's Hill.*)

> **Answer**
> *T* is the tree on the top of the hill. *SSS* is the three stones below it.

- Focus on the big picture and ask: *Who's the man?* Use the picture to introduce *wizard, cloak* and *sword.* Ask students what they think is behind the gate. (*A cave.*)
- 🔈 Play the recording (or read the text aloud if you prefer) while students listen and follow in their books.
- Elicit or explain the meaning of *explosion, appeared* and *disappeared.* Ask: *Who made the explosion?* (*Merlin.*) *What appeared after the explosion?* (*The Gate of Rings.*)
- Ask these comprehension questions and elicit answers from the class. Alternatively, you could write them on the board and ask students to write down the answers.
  1 *Who was Mr Neil?* (*Merlin.*)
  2 *How did he open the side of the hill?* (*He touched the ground with his sword.*)
  3 *Did he know how to open the Gate of Rings?* (*No, he didn't.*)
  4 *Sophie heard a voice in her head. Who was it?* (*The Red Queen.*)
  5 *Why wasn't the secret word clear in Sophie's head?* (*Because there was a strong red light in her head.*)
  6 *Something helped her to find the word. What was it?* (*The moonstone.*)
  7 *How did Sophie open the Gate of Rings?* (*She shouted the secret word.*)

- 📻 To conclude, play the recording while students follow the story in their books. Sophie has passed her 'last test' – but what is the purpose of her 'mission'? Why do the Silent Powers need her? Discuss these questions in the students' language. Remind them of Mr Neil's words about Epona: *'The king is calling her'* – what could this mean?

Puzzle tasks

- Students work on the puzzle tasks individually. Check the answers together.
- Tell the students to look at King's Hill in the picture to work out the answer to the first puzzle.

> **Answer** One tree. Three stones

- Tell the students to look at the big picture to work out the answer to the second puzzle.

> **Answer** Five rings.

- For the third puzzle, they need to look carefully at the words themselves.

> **Answer** They've got the same letters.

- Ask students to find all the words they can in the wordsquare. The secret word is the only one with five letters.

> **Answer** POWER

Extra exercises

1
> **Answers**
> 2 explorer   3 singer   4 teacher
> 5 actor/actress   6 zoologist

2
- Allow students to consult each other if they aren't sure of any information here. Point out that these people are all dead now (or in the case of the Beatles, the band no longer exists), so we must use the past simple tense.

> **Answers**
> 2 They weren't explorers. They were painters.
> 3 He wasn't a scientist. He was a pop star / singer and guitarist.
> 4 He wasn't born in Australia. He was born in Italy.
> 5 They weren't French. They were British.
> 6 She wasn't a painter. She was an actress.

3
- Students fill in the past tense forms. Ask them to suggest some more sentences about strange happenings.

> **Answers**
> 1 was   2 was   3 were   4 were   5 was   6 was

4
- Remind students of the form for past simple questions: Question word + *did* + subject + main verb.

> **Answers**
> 1 Where was Jane born?
> 2 What did she love?
> 3 Why did she save her money?
> 4 Where did she travel?
> 5 What did she watch every day?

5
- Make it clear that the questions refer to the text about Jane Goodall in Unit 11, Step 2. Tell students to look back to the text if they need to. Ask them to write their answers in complete sentences.

> **Answers**
> 1 She was born in London.
> 2 She loved animals.
> 3 She saved her money because she wanted to travel to Africa.
> 4 She travelled to Africa.
> 5 She watched chimpanzees.

6
> **Answers**
> 1 b   2 c   3 b   4 a   5 b   6 a   7 b

7
- Remind students of the difference in form between *be* and other verbs.

8
- Ask students to work on the translations in pairs or small groups, and then discuss with the whole class.

Extra reading

From North to South

BACKGROUND

At the age of ten, British-born **Robert Schumann** became the youngest person to reach the South Pole in 1992.

Spitsbergen is the largest of the group of islands that makes up the territory of Svalbard in the Arctic Ocean. It belongs to Norway.

Lead in

- Focus on the map to explain the meaning of *North Pole* and *South Pole* and ask about the weather (*It's very cold/snowy/icy/freezing.*) Write the phrase −30° C on the board, explain that we say *minus 30 degrees Celsius* and ask students to translate.
- In the students' language, ask which animals can live in the Arctic and Antarctic regions (penguins, bears, whales, foxes, seals etc.) and what people need to be able to survive.

Task

- Ask students to read the text themselves and to make a note of the words they don't know.
- Ask them to discuss the words in pairs and to try to work out their meaning from the context.
- Check their comprehension of new words. Ask them to explain or give examples of the new words if they can.
- Students read the questions and refer back to the text to find the answers.
- You can ask some further comprehension questions, using the past simple. For example:
  - *In paragraph 1, what was their 'final destination'? (The North Pole.)*
  - *What was the weather like on the trip to the North Pole? (It was cold and windy and it was snowing.)*
  - *Where did they sleep? (In sleeping bags.)*
  - *Who planned the two journeys? (Robert's father.)*

Answers

1 He was ten.
2 By plane.
3 Four.
4 When he was eleven.
5 No, they didn't. (They cycled on mountain bikes.)
6 Four.
7 He's studying at university.

Grammar: Past simple: negative, questions and short answers

Vocabulary: Time expressions

Communicative tasks:

Describing things that happened /didn't happen in the past

Writing a letter about a past event

1 Presentation *They didn't say hello*

a
- Read out the introduction to the recording. Ask about the photo and establish that Sadie, Lisa and Jack are talking in the school canteen. Focus on the pictures in the bubbles and ask: *Where were they last night?* Elicit or introduce key words from the text: *theatre, autograph, angry.*

b
- 🔊 Ask: *What was the problem?* and play the recording. Students listen with their books closed.

Answer

After the concert, the band didn't stop and say hello to their fans. They jumped into their car and disappeared.

c
- 🔊 Play the recording again while students listen and read. Explain or elicit the meaning of *enjoy.*
- Drill the three questions with *Did* and the short answers. Then drill the negative sentences in Lisa's reply: *They didn't wave ...,* etc.
- Explain the meaning of *I don't care,* and point out that Lisa is talking about her feelings now. Draw attention to her correction of Jack's statement at the end of the dialogue: not *like* but *liked* – Lisa is no longer a fan!
- Students read the sentences and choose the correct verb forms.

Answers

1 was   2 enjoyed   3 rained   4 didn't stop
5 didn't talk   6 weren't   7 liked

2 Key grammar

Past simple: questions and short answers

- Read out the questions and elicit the short answers.
- Change the subject of each question (for example, *Did the girls enjoy the concert? Did Jack get any autographs?*) and elicit the appropriate answers (*Yes, they did. No, he didn't.*).

Answers

did

No

3 Practice

- Students choose the correct answers. Tell them to look carefully at the subject of each question and to think about the tense.
- Choose students to ask and answer across the class.

Answers

1 c   2 a   3 b   4 c

As an extension for quicker students, you could add some other questions, adding the verb *be* and mixing the tenses. For example:

Are the girls in a good mood this morning? (No, they aren't.)

Was the music good at the concert? (Yes, it was.)

Did Sadie see the band after the concert? (Yes, she did.)

Was the weather nice? (No, it wasn't.)

Did the Brooklyn Boys leave in a car? (Yes, they did.)

Do they care about their fans? (No, they don't.)

Does Lisa want to see the band again? (No, she doesn't.)

4 Key grammar *Past simple: negative*

- Students complete the explanation orally and/or in writing.

Answer didn't

5 Practice

- Look at the example with the class. Students then make similar corrections by changing affirmative to negative and vice versa.
- As you go through the answers, point out the irregular past form of *say* (*said*) and practise the pronunciation /sed/.

Answers

2 She enjoyed the concert.
3 She didn't talk to the Brooklyn Boys.
4 They didn't say 'Hi! Nice to meet you.'
5 They weren't very friendly.
6 They didn't wave and smile at their fans.
7 It rained last night.
8 She was angry after the concert.

6 Writing and speaking

a ● Give students time to write their own sentences.

b ● In pairs, they ask and answer questions about last night, as in the example dialogue.

● Ask students to report two of their partner's replies, one affirmative and one negative, for example: *Stefan finished his homework, but he didn't help with the housework.*

7 Key vocabulary *Time expressions*

a ● Remind students of the time line in Unit 10 (page 102). Point out that on this time line all the expressions refer to the past.

● Ask them to write the expressions on the line in chronological order, going back into the past from 'now'.

● 📻 Play the recording for students to listen and check their answers. Draw the time line and the correct answers on the board.

● Draw attention to the expressions *yesterday morning* and *yesterday afternoon* (NOT ~~last morning~~, ~~last afternoon~~), but *last night* (NOT ~~yesterday night~~).

● Elicit one or two example sentences for each of the time expressions.

Tapescript/Answers

```
8   last year
7   last month
6   last week
5   at the weekend
4   yesterday morning
3   yesterday afternoon
2   last night
1   now
```

OPTION
You could introduce a few more past time expressions: *this morning, yesterday evening, last Wednesday, last summer, last Christmas.* Ask students to write them on the time line.

b ● Students say or write true answers to the questions.

OPTION
For further practice, write cues on the board, for example:

What / the weather like ...?
What / you / watch on TV ...?
What films / you / enjoy ...?
When / you / arrive at school ...?
When / you / finish your homework ...?
you / tidy your room ...?
you / walk to school ...?

Ask students to say the complete questions with suitable past time expressions (*What was the weather like yesterday morning?* etc.). Choose other students to reply.

8 Writing *An angry letter*

● Students refer back to the dialogue in Exercise 1 to complete Lisa's letter. This work can be done in class or set for homework.

Example answer

Dear Brooklyn Boys,

I was at your concert in Exeter last night. After the concert we waited outside in the rain. But you didn't wave or smile – you didn't even look at us. You jumped into your car and disappeared. Did you care? No, you didn't! We were your fans, but we aren't now!

From

Lisa Carter

Grammar: Past simple: irregular verbs

Communicative task: Describing events in the past

STEP 2

1 Presentation *I went to America*

BACKGROUND

John Stockwell and his family are fictional characters, but their story is based on true events.

'Pilgrim Fathers' is a 19th century name given to the founders of the Plymouth settlement at Cape Cod in Massachusetts in 1620. Some of them had been persecuted for their religious beliefs and had already left England for Holland before they set out on their voyage to the New World. They landed in December and only half their number survived the winter. After receiving help from the Native Americans, the survivors celebrated Thanksgiving after their first harvest in the autumn of 1621. Thanksgiving is still a national holiday in the USA, on the fourth Thursday in November.

Squanto, a Native American of the Patuxet tribe, had been captured by an English sea captain in 1615. He lived in England (where he learnt English) until 1619 when he was returned to North America. As well as helping the Plymouth settlers with planting and fishing, he acted as interpreter between them and the local Wampanoag tribe, who also helped them to survive.

a ● Focus on the word *went* in the exercise heading and explain that this is the past simple form of *go*. Tell students that a lot of common verbs are irregular – they don't take the normal *-ed* ending in the past simple.

● Read out the introductory paragraph and elicit the meaning of *left*. If you have a map, show the location of Plymouth in Devon and trace the *Mayflower*'s route across the Atlantic to Cape Cod, near Boston.

- Give students a few moments to look at the pictures and put them in the order they think is correct. Don't confirm or correct their answers yet (they will do this in 1b).
- Ask students to say what they can about the pictures. Use them to introduce some of the key words in the text: *ship, Atlantic, winter, die, ill, corn*.

b
- 🔊 Play the recording while students listen and read. They then match the paragraphs with the pictures.
- From the context of the words in the text, ask students to guess the meaning of *coast, survive, save somebody's life* (plural: *lives*) and *hero*.

Answers
1 d   2 c   3 a   4 f   5 e   6 b

c
- Students complete the matching task, then ask and answer the questions across the class.
- Focus on the irregular past verbs in paragraphs 4–6 and ask students to work out what the infinitive forms are.

Answers
1 f   2 e   3 c   4 a   5 d   6 g   7 b

2 Key grammar *Past simple: irregular verbs*

- Students refer back to the text and write the past simple forms.
- Drill both forms of each verb together.
- Check the students' understanding by eliciting an example sentence for each of the past tense forms. Encourage them to use past time expressions in these sentences.
- Emphasise that they will need to learn and revise the irregular forms – there are no grammatical rules for the formation of these verbs in the past simple.

Answers
1 arrived   2 left   3 came
4 spoke   5 knew   6 had

3 Practice

a
- Point out that all the sentences refer to past events from the story, so the verbs must be in the past simple.
- Students fill in the verbs in writing and compare answers with a partner. Check answers with the whole class.

Answers
2 went   3 came   4 was, spoke   5 was, saw
6 knew   7 had   8 ate

b
- Ask students to write at least one sentence of their own – more if possible. Their sentences can be about real or imaginary events.
- In pairs, students complete each other's sentences.

OPTION

You can use past simple verbs for a game of 'Bingo' (see page 103 in the Teacher's Book). Write a list on the board with past simple verbs (regular and irregular) from the unit so far. Ask students to fill out their grid with verbs from the list. When you play, call out the infinitives of the verb, so that students have to recognise the connection between the infinitive and the past form. For a second round of the game, you could reverse the procedure, so that they write infinitives and you read out past forms.

4 Key grammar
Irregular verbs: negative and questions

- Students complete the table orally and/or in writing.
- Point out that the formation of negatives and questions is the same for irregular verbs as for regular ones. Make sure students recognise that after *did/didn't* we use the infinitive (*They didn't go*, NOT ~~They didn't went~~).

Answers
didn't
go

5 Practice

- Students write the three forms of each verb.

🔊 Pattern drill: TRP, page 15, (Unit 12, Step 2).

Answers
2   She saw. She didn't see. Did she see?
3   We ate. We didn't eat. Did we eat?
4   He spoke. He didn't speak. Did he speak?
5   You had. You didn't have. Did you have?

6 Writing and speaking

- Set a time limit of five minutes. In pairs, students write as many sentences as they can. Ask them to use a range of verbs.

Example answers
They didn't have computers.
They didn't eat pizzas.
They didn't go to the cinema.
They were often hungry.

7 Listening and speaking

a ● Ask students to write a list 1–8. Tell them that they will hear eight sentences about things they did.

● 📻 Play the recording, twice if necessary. Pause briefly after each sentence to give students time to write *true* or *false*.

b ● 📻 Play each sentence again and invite different students to make a true statement (affirmative or negative) about themselves.

Tapescript

1 I had cereal for my breakfast this morning.
2 I saw my aunt and uncle on Sunday.
3 I went to the cinema on Saturday.
4 I didn't do any sport at the weekend.
5 I didn't eat any fruit yesterday.
6 I came to school on my bike this morning.
7 I left the house at eight o'clock this morning.
8 I knew how to count in English when I was at primary school.

8 Writing *My diary*

● Students choose one of the options. You could ask them to subdivide their day(s) into times (Saturday morning/ afternoon, etc.) and to plan their work by making notes under these headings. If they choose the 'imaginary day', encourage them to be as imaginative as they like.

● Draw attention to the list of irregular verbs on page 143 and to verbs that they may find useful, for example: *bought, drove, got (up), made, met, read.*

● The writing can be completed for homework.

Example answers

On Saturday morning I went shopping and I bought some new shoes. I had lunch at home. In the afternoon Kate came and we went for a walk by the river. In the evening we watched a video and Kate stayed at my house. On Sunday … (etc.)

Or:

On Saturday morning I arrived in Washington. I went to the White House and the President met me in the Oval Office. I had lunch with him in his apartment, but we had an argument and I left. In the afternoon I decided to go to New York … (etc.)

OPTION

For this final unit of the Student's Book, ask students to devise their own Try this! puzzle, looking back through Try this! boxes in previous units for ideas. They can exchange puzzles with several different partners.

Communicative tasks:
Talking about holidays
Talking about your school year

1 Reading *Jetline Oz*

a ● Elicit or explain the meaning of *advert*. Ask students to read the advert quickly to get a general sense of what it is about and answer the question. Ask them where we can see adverts like this. (*In newspapers and magazines.*)

● Help students to guess the meaning of *best, prices, flights* and *book* (verb). Do they know what *24/7* means? (24 hours a day, 7 days a week – in other words, all the time.)

● If you have a map, you can show the location of Perth and Melbourne. Practise the pronunciation: /pɛːθ/ and /ˈmelbən/.

Answer c

b ● Students read the sentences and fill in the missing words orally and/or in writing.

Answers
1 Sydney, Perth, Melbourne
2 €799 3 book 4 open

2 Listening *Song*

a ● 📻 Ask the questions and play the song. Students listen for the answers.

Answers
To Sydney.   On Sunday.

b ● Read out the sentences and ask students to complete the matching task.

● Elicit the meaning of *pack*. Remind students that *bought* is the past of *buy*, and practise the pronunciation /bɔːt/.

Answers
1 c 2 e 3 f 4 a 5 d 6 b

c ● Ask students to pick out the verb in each sentence. They then put the sentences in the right lists.

● 📻 You could play the song again and ask students to listen for the days. Ask: *He's singing about days in the past and the future – what day is it today?* (Saturday.)

● 📻 Ask students to turn to the song words on page 144. Play the song once again and encourage them to join in.

Answers
The past: 1, 2, 3, 4
The future: 5, 6

3 Key pronunciation
Words with the same sound

- Ask students to read the list themselves first.
- Play the recording. Students listen and repeat.
- They then list the words according to their vowel sound. You could write up the phonetic symbols for the three vowels: /æ/, /ɔ/ and /ʌ/.
- Check answers together. Play the recording again if there are any disagreements on pronunciation.

> **Answers**
> 1 bag, black, hand, catch, sad, flat
> 2 bought, walk, short, door, hall, floor
> 3 fun, come, lunch, love, month, rug

4 Speaking
The past and the future

- Ask students to think about their first term at secondary school, and the things they enjoyed and didn't enjoy.
- Ask a student to read out the first example. Ask which tense is used (past simple).
- Ask students to think about their ideal summer holiday.
- Ask a student to read out the example. Ask why *going to* is used. (Because we are talking about future plans.)
- Students can work in pairs, telling their ideas to each other, then share their ideas with the whole class.

CHAPTER 10   The Silent Powers
A horse for the king's men

> The legendary **King Arthur** was a chivalric hero who ruled from his court at Camelot with the support of his Knights of the Round Table. The stories tell of Arthur's valiant defence of the kingdom, of the love between his queen, Guinevere, and his bravest knight, Sir Lancelot; of the search for the Holy Grail (Christ's cup from the Last Supper and the symbol of perfection) and of Arthur's death at the hands of his nephew. These are medieval legends, but there probably was a real Arthur – perhaps a powerful British chieftain who resisted the forces of the invading Saxons in the 6th century.

- Remind students of the events in Chapter 9. You could read out the following quotes and ask: Who said this?
  - 'Mr Neil? Is It you?' (Sophie.)
  - 'Now we must open the Gate of Rings' (Merlin.)
  - 'You can never open the gate!' (The Red Queen.)
  Ask: *How did Sophie open the gate? What was the secret word?* (Power.)

- Focus on the picture and ask students what they can see. Use them to introduce key words in the text: *knights, crown, box, necklace*. Point out the silent *k* in *knight*.
- Play the recording (or read the text) while students listen and follow in their books.
- Ask them to say where Sophie was at the beginning and at the end of the chapter. Elicit or explain the meaning of *rich, destruction, ordinary*.
- You could ask students to find all the past simple verbs in the text and to give the infinitive forms. When they come to the new verb *found*, ask them to guess what the infinitive is. Teach the new verb *fall* with its irregular past form *fell*.
- Ask these true/false questions to check comprehension.
  1 The knights were all asleep. (True.)
  2 King Arthur wasn't there. (False. He was in the middle of the cave, asleep.)
  3 All the knights had a horse. (False. One knight didn't have a horse.)
  4 Sophie must leave Epona and the moonstone in the cave. (True.)
  5 Sophie's gift from King Arthur was a necklace of ten stones. (False. It was a necklace of nine stones.)
  6 When Sophie came out of the cave she saw an ordinary hill – there was no gate or cave. (True.)
  7 We know how Sophie got from King's Hill to London. (False. We don't know)
  8 When Sophie went into her flat, a key was on the floor. (False. There was a letter.)
- To conclude, play the recording while students follow the story in their books. Invite students to suggest ideas about the contents of the letter, and about the way the story might end.

Puzzle tasks

- Students work on the puzzle tasks individually.
- Tell the students to look at Merlin's speech to work out what KKKKK x 20 refers to.

> **Answer** 100 knights.

- Students look back at the meaning of the runes and complete the poem. Ask them to practise reading it aloud.
- Ask them to 'interpret' the poem by recalling events in the story. For example, *Where did Sophie's journey start and where did it end? What was the importance of her dream? Who was in the team that helped her work out the mystery? What gift did she receive? How did she show her power?*

Extra exercises

1 ● If students have trouble with any of these verbs, remind them that there is a list of irregular verbs on page 143 of the Student's Book.

Answers

2 saw 3 spoke 4 ate 5 had 6 left, was

2

Answers

1 c 2 b 3 a 4 b 5 a 6 c 7 a

3 ● Point out that the questions are all referring to a holiday in the past. Ask students to write their answers in full sentences.

Example answers

1 I went to Thailand.
2 I went with my friend Ruth and her family.
3 Yes, it was.
4 We ate curry, fish and Thai salad.
5 Yes, I did. It was fantastic.

4 ● Check that students understand that all the sentences are false and must be corrected.

Answers

2 Lisa didn't get their autographs.
3 Jack didn't go to the concert.
4 John Stockwell wasn't born in America.
5 His sister Mary didn't die in France.
6 At first, the Pilgrim Fathers didn't have a lot of food.

5

Answers

1 a 2 c 3 b 4 a 5 b

6 ● Ask students to work on the translations in pairs or small groups, and then discuss with the whole class.

Extra reading

Quiz: The UK and the USA

Task

● Read out the quiz questions and help with new vocabulary (*states, prime minister, independence, female, flag* etc.). For question 7, make sure that students are aware that America was a British colony before they fought a war to gain their independence.

● Ask students to go through the quiz and choose the answers they think are correct. Allow them to discuss their answers in pairs or small groups before you check with the whole class.

● Discuss the answers with the class. Ask questions to elicit extra information, for example:

1 Which state is separated from the rest of the USA by Canada?
2 What are the four countries?
3 Where's Hollywood? Where's the Statue of Liberty?
4 Who lives at Buckingham Palace? Where does the US president live?
6 What was the name of their ship?
7 Were the British happy to give America independence?
8 Who is the prime minister now?
9 Who is the president now, and who is his wife?
10 Which country's flag is the stars and stripes? How many stars are there on the flag?

Answers

1 c
2 a (England, Scotland, Wales and Northern Ireland)
3 c
4 a (The Queen lives in Buckingham Palace.)
5 b (It is thought that the first North Americans crossed the Bering Straits from Asia and settled.)
6 b
7 a (4th July is still celebrated in thee US as Independence Day.)
8 a (Margaret Thatcher was UK prime minister from 1979 to 1990.)
9 c
10 b (The Stars and Stripes is the name of the US flag. The St. George's Cross is the flag of England.)

1   You could extend the quiz by reading out true/false sentences using past and present tenses. Students decide whether they are true or false and correct the false sentences if they can.

   – *In the UK and the USA, cars drive on the left. (False. In the USA they drive on the right.)*
   – *The first president of the USA was George Washington. (True.)*
   – *The river in london is called the Thames. (True.)*
   – *The Golden Gate Bridge is in New York. (False. It's in San Francisco.)*
   – *The Americans bought Alaska from Spain. (False. They bought it from Russia.)*
   – *The capital of Scotland is Glasgow. (False. The capital is Edinburgh.)*
   – *The English King Henry VIII had six wives. (True.)*
   – *Spanish people went to America before British people. (True.)*
   – *In the 13th century, most people in England spoke French. (True.)*
   – *The sea between the UK and the USA is the Pacific Ocean. (False. It's the Atlantic Ocean.)*

2   You may want to point out some differences between British and American English words. Ask students to use dictionaries to match the following words and write them under the headings *British English* and *American English*. Check to make sure that the meanings are clear.

   underground   cookies   apartment   sweets elevator   flat   candy   subway   lift pavement   sidewalk   biscuits

   Get students to write the two lists of words on the board:

British English:	American English:
underground	subway
biscuits	cookies
flat	apartment
sweets	candy
lift	elevator
pavement	sidewalk

Module 6 Review

Language summary

1 Past simple: *was/were*

1.1 ● Choose pairs of students to say the dialogue across the room, and then to substitute other words for the ones underlined. For example:

A: *Where were you at 5.30 last Tuesday?*

B: *I was at home.*

A: *No, you weren't.*

B: *Yes, I was. Ask my parents. They were with me.*

● In pairs, students practise the dialogue, making their own substitutions.

Answers

were; was; No; Yes; was

1.2 ● When students have completed the questions, ask for the answers. If they don't know, invite them to make suggestions.

Answers

1 The Colossus was in Rhodes, Greece.
2 Where was Cleopatra's palace?
  It was in Alexandria.
3 Who was Julius Caesar?
  He was a Roman soldier and politician/leader.
4 Who were the Marx Brothers?
  They were comic actors.
5 What was Apollo 11?
  It was a spaceship that went to the moon.
6 When were the first Olympic Games?
  The first modern Olympics were in 1896.

2 There was/were

● Elicit or explain the meaning of *pets* and *pupils*.
● Ask students to write their own answers to the questions.

Answers

2 Were there   3 Was there   4 Was there
5 Were there   6 Were there   7 Were there

3 Past simple: regular and irregular verbs

3.1 ● Elicit or explain the meaning of the new vocabulary: *Father Christmas, cartoons, relatives*. Remind students of the use of *believe in*, meaning 'to believe that something exists'.

● Warn them that some of the verbs in the list are regular and others are irregular.

Answers

2 believed   3 went   4 watched
5 ate   6 visited   7 wanted

3.2 ● Students make true sentences about themselves, using the negative form of the verbs.

3.3 ● Remind students of the form for past simple questions: (question word +) *did* + subject + main verb. Point out that this is the same for regular and irregular verbs.

Answers

1   When did Jane leave England?
2   Why did she go to Africa?
3   Where did Jack live?
4   Did the native Americans help the Pilgrims?
5   What language did they speak?
6   Did Lisa enjoy the concert?

4 Time expressions

Example answers

Our teacher was late this morning.
I visited my cousin yesterday afternoon.
My pen friend wrote to me last week.

5 Past simple of *have / have got*

● Look at the examples with the class. Emphasise that the past form of *have/has got* is *had* (NOT ~~had got~~).

● You could extend the point to the negative and question forms, For example, compare these sentences:

Present:

He's got a cat.

He hasn't got a cat.

Has he got a cat?

Past:

He had a cat.

He didn't have a cat. (NOT ~~hadn't got~~)

Did he have a cat? (NOT ~~Had he got~~)

● Students change the sentences from the present to the past.

Study skills 6   Planning your learning

- Read through the list and discuss the strategies with the class. In what ways could these be useful? Can they think of other strategies that will help them to learn, remember and use the language?
- For the vocabulary notebook and the vocabulary cards, remind students of the methods of recording new words that were suggested in Study skills 4 (page 90).
- Invite students to state their intentions for the future, using *going to*.

How's it going?

Your rating

- Students look back at the exercises in the Language summary and make their own assessment of how well they understand and remember the material.

Vocabulary

- Encourage students to choose words that they might have trouble remembering, and to try to write sentences that show the meaning of the words.

Test a friend

- Look at the example questions and elicit the correct answers.
- Students refer back to the texts in Units 11 and 12 and write several questions to test their partner. They then ask and answer in pairs.

Write to your teacher

- In this final letter, invite students to say how they feel about their course. Encourage them to be honest about the things they enjoyed and didn't enjoy. Reading this feedback should help you to reflect on your teaching methodology and may suggest improvements that you could make in the future.

OPTION

If you have any comments you would like to make (or pass on from your students), we would be delighted to hear from you. So, if you have time, please write to us and let us know how you got on with *Messages*.

Your Workbook

- Students should complete a Learning diary when they come to the end of each unit.

Coursework   All about me!

My life line

Students write about important events in their lives.

BACKGROUND

In a **nativity play**, primary school children act out the Christmas story, usually before an audience of parents and relatives, just before the school breaks up for the Christmas holiday.

Comprehensive schools are secondary schools which are open to local students of all abilities – there is no 'academic' entrance requirement.

Friends of the Earth is a 'green' organisation which aims to protect the natural environment. It operates worldwide.

Dartmoor is a national park of rugged and spectacular hills and moorland in southwest England.

- Give students a few minutes to look at Jack's 'life line'. Point out that these are events that were important personally for Jack – including sad and difficult experiences as well as happy ones.
- Ask students to read the text and match the photos, badges etc. to the events in the time line.
- Go through the text and help with new vocabulary.
- Ask students to pick out the past simple verbs in Jack's text and to say if they are regular or irregular. Elicit the infinitive forms of the verbs.
- Invite students to talk about a few of the past events that are important to them. Encourage a range of suggestions, to help stimulate ideas.
- Ask students to jot down notes about events they remember. They then choose the ones they want to put on their time line and think about the illustrations they can use.
- Set a time limit for work on the project. The work should mainly be done at home.

OPTION

At the end of the course you could ask each student to display all six of their Coursework pages in a folder or scrapbook. These could be displayed in the classroom, for students to look at and read each other's Coursework.

Games

Simon says

Ask students to stand up and listen to your instructions. If you say *Simon says ...* at the beginning of the instruction, the students must do the action, but if you don't say it, they must keep still. If they do the wrong thing or follow an instruction without *Simon says*, they are 'out' and have to sit down. Keep the pace brisk and increase the speed as you go. The winner is the last student left standing.

This game is especially useful for things in the classroom, parts of the body, action verbs and prepositions. Instructions can include: *Point to ..., Touch ..., Look at ..., Hold up ..., Put down ..., Close/Open (your eyes, your book), Clap your hands, Wave your hand, Stand up, Sit down, Put ... on / under / in front of ...* .

Noughts and crosses

Divide the class into two teams (0 and X) and make a grid of nine squares on the board. In the example below, the squares are filled in with prepositions, but you can use any set of vocabulary or, for example, a set of verbs to be used in a certain tense, a set of adjectves to be turned into their opposites, a mixture of countable and uncountable nouns to be used with *some* or *any*, etc.

on	under	in front of
in the middle of	opposite	in
behind	above	next to

The first student on the 0 team must choose a preposition and use it in a sentence. If the sentence is correct and true, rub out the preposition and replace it with *0*. It is then the X team's turn to choose one of the remaining prepositions and make a sentence. The winners are the first team to make a line of three *0*s or three *X*s, either horizontally, vertically or diagonally.

Bingo

Students draw a grid of nine squares and fill them in with nine words belonging to a certain set. (The set of words must be larger than nine.) These could be numbers, classroom words, clothes, food and drink, past tense verb forms, adjectives etc., or they could be words from a reading or listening text. Call out words from the set, keeping a record of the ones you have used. When students hear a word in their grid, they cross it out. The first person to cross out all their words calls out *Bingo!* and wins the game.

Picture memory game

Use a picture or photo in the Student's Book as the basis for a memory game. Target language could include *is/are* + prepositions or colours, *There is/are, have/has got* or the present continuous.

Divide the class into two teams and ask them to look at the picture. They then close their books. Team A and B students take it in turns to say a true sentence about the photo. You are the adjudicator – refer to the book to check the answers and award points. If a student's answer is correct, the team scores a point. If the answer is incorrect or repeats a previous answer, the team gets nothing.

Word tennis

You can revise vocabulary by choosing sets of words that the students have learnt (clothes, animals, places in a town, geographical features etc.). In pairs, students 'serve' and 'return' words to each other within two or three seconds (for example: *jacket – shirt, hat – coat, gloves – socks* etc.) until one person runs out of ideas or repeats a word that has already been said. If appropriate, you can invite two confident students to play against each other in front of the class. Students then change partners and play again with a different vocabulary set.

Jeopardy

Prepare 12 questions on a particular category (numbers, adjective opposites, plural nouns etc.) and put the questions in envelopes (for example: *What's the opposite of 'hot'? What's the opposite of 'expensive'?*) each with a number (1–12) and a points total clearly visible on the outside. Divide the class into two teams. Write the category on the board and attach the 12 envelopes underneath. Team leaders take it in turn to pick an envelope, and the team has a few moments to confer before the leader answers the question. If the answer is correct, the team receives the number of points on the envelope. If it is incorrect, the points are deducted from their score.

Coffeepot

For verb practice. One student thinks of a common action (write an email, ride a bike, clean my teeth, do my homework etc.). The others have to guess the action by asking questions, substituting the word *coffeepot* for the verb. For example:

Do you coffeepot every day?

Do people usually coffeepot outside?

Where do you coffeepot?

Did you coffeepot this morning?

When did you last coffeepot?

Are you going to coffeepot this afternoon? (etc.)

Workbook key and tapescripts

1 What do you remember?

1 a 2 cat 3 apple 4 pizza 5 bag 6 notebook
7 banana 8 desk 9 elephant

b *Animals:* dog, cat, elephant
Food: apple, pizza, banana
In the classroom: bag, notebook, desk

2 Check individual answers.

3 2 f 3 b 4 c 5 d 6 a

4 2 I'm fine, thanks.
3 My name's Roberto.
4 What is it?
5 It's an apple.
6 I like animals.

5 *Puzzle:*
1 Friday 2 Monday 3 Thursday
4 Sunday 5 Tuesay 6 Saturday
7 Wednesday

September:
7 Tuesday 8 Wednesday 9 Thursday
10 Friday 11 Saturday 12 Sunday

6 Check individual answers.

1 1 I don't know.
2 I know.
3 Pardon? Can you say that again?
4 What does it mean?
5 Can you help me, please?

2 2 close 3 look 4 listen
5 read 6 write 7 ask 8 answer

3 2 Open your book/dictionary.
3 Close your book/dictionary.
4 Look at your dictionary / the pictures / the board / your book.
5 Read the sentences.
6 Listen to the CD/song.
7 Ask a friend.
8 Make a list.

4 1 He's 2 Her 3 His 4 She's

5 2 c 3 c 4 a 5 c

6 2 Sadie 3 Sadie (and) Jack 4 Joe 5 Kate
6 Jack 7 Kate 8 Joe

1 2 a 3 d 4 c 5 b

2 2nd – second 3rd – third 4th – fourth 5th – fifth
6th – sixth 7th – seventh 8th – eighth 9th – ninth
10th – tenth

3 2 Y 3 C 4 I 5 A 6 R

4 2 b ✓ 3 a ✓ 4 b ✓ 5 a ✓ 6 b ✓

TAPESCRIPT
1 thirteen
2 D
3 forty
4 N
5 eighty
6 W

5 2 Can I read your letter?
3 Can I look at your photos?
4 How do you spell 'Liverpool'?
5 How do you say 'carne' in English?

6 Can I open the window?

2 Are you ready?

1 1 keyboard player 2 singer 3 guitarists 4 drummer
5 called 6 members 7 leader
The leader is: Joe Kelly.

2 2 name's 3 Adriana's 4 She's 5 We're
6 She's, I'm 7 They're

3 2 It's, Monsoon
3 She's, singer
4 They're, guitarists
5 She's, drummer
6 He's, keyboard player

4 ... my friends call me <u>Mel</u>
I'm fourteen. I'm English.
I'm a <u>student</u> ...
It<u>'s</u> in <u>Exeter</u>.

For the second part, check individual answers.

5 2 How 3 What 4 Where 5 Who 6 When
2 c 3 d 4 b 5 a 6 e

6

HELEN: Hello. Is that Mel Adams?

MEL: Yes.

HELEN: My name's Helen. I'm in Class 10B. I'm a singer.

MEL: Great! We need another singer in the band. Come to the next practice.

HELEN: When is it?

MEL: It's tomorrow.

HELEN: Where is it?

MEL: In room 12.

HELEN: OK. See you tomorrow.

STEP 2

1 1 b 2 a 3 b 4 b

2 2 isn't 3 's 4 aren't 5 're
6 'm not, 'm [nationality] 7 are

3 2 Are your friends at Westover School?
3 Are they in your class?
4 Is he your English teacher?
5 Am I in Group 1 or Group 2?
6 Are we late?
7 Is Liverpool in Australia?
8 Is it in England?

4 2 Emma is from Australia. Emma's English. Emma is from England.
3 He's 15. He's 14.
4 They aren't interested in computers. They're interested in computers.

TAPESCRIPT

1 JUSTIN: Hi! I'm Justin. I'm from Jamaica. I'm thirteen. I'm very good at sport.
2 EMMA: Hello. I'm Emma. I'm English. I'm twelve. I'm good at music.
3 DAN: Hi. I'm Dan. I'm fourteen. I'm Australian. I'm interested in animals.
4 MARTHA: Hi! I'm Martha.
MIKE: And I'm Mike. We're from New York. We're fourteen.
MARTHA: We're interested in computers and we're very good at science.

5 2 science 3 music 4 cooking 5 computer games
6 art 7 swimming 8 reading

For the second part, check individual answers.

6 2 Is; No, he isn't.
3 Are; Yes, I am / No, I'm not.
4 Are; Yes, we are. / No, we aren't.
5 Are; Yes, they are.
6 Are; No, they aren't.
7 Is; No, it isn't.
8 Is; Yes, it is.

7 2 and 3 and 4 but 5 but 6 and

8 2 He's quite good at / not bad at
3 He isn't very good at
4 He's quite good at / not bad at
5 He's very good at

9 Check individual answers.

STEP 3

1 2 rivers 3 mountains 4 volcanoes
5 countries 6 lakes

2 1 are 2 isn't 3 is 4 isn't 5 aren't 6 are, is

3 Check individual answers.

3 What have you got?

STEP 1

1 2 umbrella 3 crisps 4 tissues 5 pencil case 6 key
7 tennis racket 8 watch 9 anorak 10 badge

2 2 a, a, some 3 an, some, an 4 some
5 a 6 an

3 2 some, any 3 any 4 any 5 any 6 some, any
7 any 8 some

4 1 got 2 have/'ve got, haven't got
3 have got, they haven't got

5 2 Have you got a calculator? Yes, I have. / No, I haven't.
3 Have Sadie and Lisa got any tissues? Yes, they have.
4 Have Joe and Sadie got a tortoise? Yes, they have.
5 Have they got a snake? No, they haven't.
6 Have you got a dictionary? Yes, I have. / No, I haven't.

6 Hi! My name's Ross Kennedy. I'm Canadian and I'm thirteen years old. I've got a sister, but I haven't got any brothers. We've got a cat and two dogs. What about you? Have you got any pets? My favourite music is hip-hop and I like skateboarding. Have you got a skateboard? Have you got any computer games?
Write soon!
Ross

7 Check individual answers.

STEP 2

1 2 Joe's keyboard 3 Lisa's umbrella
4 Sadie's socks 5 Barney's sandwiches
6 Mrs Kelly's letters

2

	is	possessive
2	He's	Sadie's
3	Kate's	Sadie and Joe's
4	It's	Sadie's
5	Lisa's	Sadie's
6	What's	dog's

3   2 His   3 Her   4 Their   5 our   6 Her

4   1 b   2 c   3 a   4 a

5   2 Is that   3 Are these   4 Are those

6   2 b   3 d   4 g   5 h   6 f   7 a   8 e

STEP 3

1   **a**   2 mother   3 husband   4 daughter   5 sister
        6 uncle   7 children

     b   1 aunt   2 uncle   3 parents   4 children
        5 grandmother   6 grandfather   7 cousin
        8 son   9 daughter   10 wife

2   A = 5   C = 3   D = 4   E = 2

TAPESCRIPT

1 These are my parents.
2 This is me with my husband
   and my husband's brother.
3 This is me with my parents. I haven't
   got any brothers or sisters.
4 This is my aunt and uncle and my
   two cousins.
5 This is me with my brother and
   my sister.

3   *Father:* a wife and four children
     Mother: a husband and four children
     Brother: a father, a mother and three sisters
     Lauren: a father, a mother, two sisters and a brother

4   **Descriptions**

STEP 1

1   2 big, small   3 difficult, easy   4 noisy, quiet
     5 happy, sad   6 new, old   7 boring, exciting
     8 good, bad

2   2 What are they like?
     3 What's he like?
     4 What's it like?
     5 What are they like?
     6 What's she like?

3   2 Is sky surfing a dangerous sport?
     3 Who's your favourite pop star?
     4 He's an awful dancer.
     5 I live in a noisy city.
     6 I've got a serious problem.

4   **a**   Pictures F, A, B, D and I.

     b   *Luke:* quiet music, serious TV programmes, old cars,
        sad films

5   1 ... an American city.
     2 ... a famous book and a film.
     3 ... an exciting sport.
     4 ... an English city.
     5 ... a small car.
     6 ... a funny TV programme.

STEP 2

1   **a**   A = Tom   B = Pete   C = Harry   D = Sam

     b   1 friendly   2 nice   3 happy   4 kind

2   2 She's got a long nose.
     3 We've got blue eyes.
     4 I've got short legs.
     5 They've got white T-shirts.
     6 You've got a red face.

3   2 They haven't got a map.
     3 He hasn't got a surfboard.
     4 They haven't got an umbrella.

4   2 Has Tina got
     3 Has Tom got
     4 Have Tina and Tanya got
     5 Yes, he has.
     6 Yes, she has.
     7 No, they haven't.
     8 No, she hasn't.

5   1 c   2 b   3 a   4 c

TAPESCRIPT

SADIE: Pete, have you got any brothers and sisters?
PETE: Yes, I've got a sister. I haven't got any
   brothers.
SADIE: What's your sister's name?
PETE: Helen. She's thirteen.
SADIE: What's she like?
PETE: She's quite tall. She's got long, fair hair.
   She's very good at sport.
SADIE: Have you got any pets?
PETE: Yes, I've got a snake and my sister has got
   a cat.
SADIE: A snake! What's its name?
PETE: Sidney.

6   **a**   Picture B.

     b   2 It's very friendly ✓
        4 It's got a name ✓

1

```
H E A R T P F
A Y R I A O A
N E M O R T C
D M O U T H E
Y B N O S E T
F O O T T A O
A B L E G D M
```

Answers may be in any order.

2 hand 3 eye 4 arm 5 face 6 mouth
7 head 8 nose 9 leg 10 foot

2 2 heavy 3 heart 4 empty 5 aeroplane 6 fed up

3
2 She's got (a) stomach ache.
3 We're fine.
4 You're tired.
5 They're fed up.
6 Joe's got / Joe has got a headache.

4 2 long 3 happiness 4 empty 5 tall 6 teacher
7 apple 8 quiet

5 My world

1 The following words should be crossed out:
2 magazines 3 the Internet
4 lemonade 5 a meal 6 tomato ketchup
7 an umbrella 8 a TV programme

2 2 go 3 go 4 read 5 watch 6 listen 7 like
8 write 9 use 10 eat

3
2 He goes to Marsden College.
3 He goes to a basketball club (every Friday).
4 He reads a lot of magazines.
5 After school he watches TV.
6 He listens to music.
7 He likes rap.
8 He writes emails (to his friends).
9 He uses the Internet.
10 He eats a lot of pizza.

4 2 come 3 like 4 likes 5 loves
6 prefers 7 play 8 prefer

5 2 eats 3 goes 4 comes 5 watches 6 uses

6
3 False. Sadie and Jack learn French at school.
4 False. Jack doesn't watch sport on TV.
5 False. Sadie doesn't like horror films.
6 True.
7 False. Sadie and Jack don't watch sport on TV.
8 False. Sadie plays a musical instrument.

7 Check individual answers.

1 2 g 3 a 4 e 5 d 6 c 7 b

2 2 Do 3 Does 4 Have 5 Do 6 Are 7 Are
Martin is scared of <u>rats</u>.

3 a
2 Does Joe like vegetables? (use)
3 Does Joe play football and basketball? (Internet)
4 Do Joe and Sadie like music? (does)
5 Do you speak French? (the)

b 6 Does Sadie use the Internet?

c
2 No, he doesn't.
3 Yes, he does.
4 Yes, they do.
5 Yes, I do. / No, I don't.
6 Yes, she does.

4
Line 1: spider
Line 2: alien
Line 3: thunder
Line 4: shark
Line 5: ghost
Line 6: rats
Line 8: UFO, bats

5 2 comics 3 horror film 4 glass 5 tourists

6

	Television	Sport	Computers	Books	Music
1 Tom	✓	✗	✓	✗	✓
2 Anna	✗	✓	✓	✓	✓
3 Rick	✓	✓	✗	✓	✓

TAPESCRIPT

1 I'm Tom. I listen to music. I play computer games. I don't read books. I watch television. I don't like sport.

2 My name's Anna. I play tennis and basketball. I play the piano every day. I like science fiction books. I write a lot of emails to my friends, and I use the Internet. I don't watch television.

3 I'm Rick. I love music and sport. I think computers are boring. I watch TV, but I prefer reading. I love books.

7 Example answers
Tom doesn't like sport. He doesn't read books.
Anna likes books. She uses a computer.
Rick doesn't like computers. He watches TV.

1 2 What 3 What sort of 4 Who 5 Where
6 When 7 Why

2 2 g 3 c 4 a 5 d 6 f 7 b

3 Check individual answers.

6 I'm usually late!

1

2 snake 3 bear 4 dolphin 5 tortoise 6 cat
7 lion 8 giraffe 9 gorilla 10 rat 11 dog
12 shark

2 2 usually 3 sometimes 4 usually 5 sometimes
6 never 7 often 8 don't often

3 Check individual answers.

4 2 He doesn't often tidy his room.   Picture E
3 Are you always hungry?   Picture D
4 Emma isn't always happy.   Picture C
5 He never cleans his bike.   Picture G
6 Do you usually sleep on the floor? Picture A
7 Louise is sometimes late for school. Picture F

5 2 c 3 a 4 f 5 b 6 e

6 Check individual answers.

1 **a** Picture A = Ben   Picture C = Joe   Picture D = Sadie

b Mr Kelly has sandwiches and salad. Then he has yoghurt.
He drinks coffee.

2 1 c 2 b 3 b 4 a 5 c 6 b

TAPESCRIPT

CANTEEN LADY: Hello, Mel. What do you want?

MEL: Er … a vegetarian pizza and a green salad,
please. And a banana yoghurt.

CANTEEN LADY: And what about you, Barney?

BARNEY: Er … ham and chips, please, and a
fruit salad. And a can of lemonade.

CANTEEN LADY: Hello, Lee. What do you want?

LEE: Er … chicken curry and a can of apple juice,
please. Oh, and a banana.

3 2 have 3 has 4 has 5 Does, have 6 do, have
7 have 8 do, have

4 2 False. 3 True. 4 True. 5 False. 6 True.

5

Lunchbox A	Lunchbox B
a cheese sandwich	a chicken sandwich
a packet of crisps	a packet of peanuts
an apple	two bananas
a bottle of water	a can of lemonade

A is Sadie's lunchbox. B is Joe's lunchbox.

6 Check individual answers.

1 2 five past eleven
3 quarter past nine
4 twenty to eleven
5 twelve o'clock
6 five to twelve
7 half past seven
8 quarter to five
9 twenty-five to four
10 twenty-five past one

2 **a** A = 5 B = 8 C = 4 E = 3 F = 7 G = 6 H = 2

b 2 He has a shower at twenty past seven.
3 He has breakfast at twenty to eight.
4 He catches the bus at quarter past eight.
5 He gets to school at twenty to nine.
6 He gets home at half past four.
7 He does his homework at half past seven.
8 He goes to bed at half past ten.

c 1 does 2 When 3 What

3 Check individual answers.

7 At home

1 1 bedroom 2 bathroom 3 garden 4 upstairs
5 kitchen 6 hall 7 living room 8 dining room
9 shower 10 downstairs

2 **a** 1 61 2 swimming pool 3 four tennis courts
4 music room 5 video club

b 2 There are sixty-one teachers.
3 There's a sports hall and a swimming pool.
4 There are two gyms and four tennis courts.
5 There's a music room and two computer rooms.
6 There's a music club and a video club.

TAPESCRIPT

MAN: Sadie, how many students are there at
Westover School?

SADIE: There are nine hundred and eighty.

MAN: And how many teachers are there?

SADIE: There are sixty-one.

MAN: And what about facilities? Is there a sports
hall?

SADIE: Yes, there is. And there's a swimming pool,
two gyms and four tennis courts.

MAN: Have you got a computer room at the
school?

SADIE: We've got two computer rooms, and we've
got a big music room.

MAN: And are there any activities after school?

SADIE: Yes, there are. There are a lot of clubs. There
are sports clubs, and there's a music club and a
video club.

3 2 F 3 ? 4 T 5 ? 6 T 7 T 8 F

4
2 There aren't any good programmes on TV tonight.
3 There's a pizza in the kitchen.
4 ... there isn't a key.
5 There are two cinemas near here.

5 Check individual answers.

1
3 There's a
4 There are some
5 There's a
6 There are some
7 There's an
8 There are some

2
2 Yes, there are.
3 Is there a surfboard? Yes, there is.
4 Are there any trainers? No, there aren't.
5 Are there any baseball caps? Yes, there are.
6 Is there a guitar? No, there isn't.
7 Are there any umbrellas? No, there aren't.
8 Is there an octopus? Yes, there is.

3 a
a bottle of water   some butter
an onion   some eggs
an apple   some tomatoes
                      some cheese
                      some bread

b
2 There's some bread.
3 There's an apple.
4 There's some cheese.
5 There's a can of lemonade.
6 There's some milk.
7 There are some eggs.

4
2 ... any eggs.
3 ... there isn't any bread.
4 ... there isn't any pasta.
5 ... there aren't any apples.
6 ... there isn't any paper.

5 Check individual answers.

1
There's a lamp on the table.
1 desk 2 mirror 3 shelves 4 wardrobe
5 rug 6 clock 7 chair 8 chest of drawers

2
2 There's a bat on the wall.
3 There's a spider above the bed.
4 There's a dog opposite the woman.
5 There's a man behind the door.
6 There's a shark in the swimming pool.
7 There's a ghost next to the woman.
8 There's an elephant in front of the car.

3 Check individual answers.

8 Having fun

1
2 He can't dance.
3 She can't speak Chinese.
4 She can't ride a horse.
5 She can play the guitar.
6 He can't play football.
7 He can't swim.
8 She can sing.
9 They can fly.

2
2 Can you speak Arabic? Yes, I can. / No, I can't.
3 Can Joe play the keyboard? Yes, he can.
4 Can Mel Adams sing? Yes, she can.
5 Can you ride a horse? Yes, I can. / No, I can't.
6 Can horses fly? No, they can't.

3
2 Three years old. 3 Five years old. 4 Six weeks old
5 Two years old. 6 Four years old.

4
I'm an aeroplane.

5
1 They can swim.
2 They can't play tennis.
3 She can write. She can ride a bike.
4 He can ride a horse. He can play the piano.

1
2 shopping centre 3 station 4 Internet café
5 bus station 6 museum 7 cinema 8 park
9 aquarium 10 sports centre

2
2 They can't go swimming ...
3 They can't go shopping ...
4 They can't see a film ...
5 They can't go for a walk ...
6 They can't surf the Internet ...

3
2 You can't ride a bike here.
3 You can play basketball here.
4 You can't ride a horse here.
5 You can eat here.
6 You can't swim here.
7 You can't use a mobile phone here.
8 You can dive here.

4
1 Sue: e 2 Andy: h 3 Louise: d
4 Dan: a 5 Martha: g

TAPESCRIPT

1 GIRL: Sue, look! Can you see that blue T-shirt? Do you like it?

2 BOY: Come on, Andy. That's our train. Have you got the tickets?

3 GIRL: Wow! Louise! Look at the sharks! Do you think they eat the other fish?

4 GIRL: What are these, Dan?

BOY: They're sharks' teeth. They're two thousand years old!

5   **BOY:** Martha, who's the man in the red T-shirt?
      GIRL: He's the woman's husband.
      PERSON: Ssssh!

5
2 I can see a man's face. [See left of tree.]
3 I can see a train.
4 I can't see any cars.
5 I can see a plane.
6 I can't see a horse.
7 I can see some birds.

6
2 <u>Can</u> you <u>hear</u> that music?
3 I <u>can't see</u> the television.
4 <u>Can</u> you <u>see</u> my anorak?
5 I <u>can't hear</u> my CD.
6 I <u>can hear</u> you, but I <u>can't see</u> you.

7
Check individual answers.

1
2 You mustn't interrupt me.
3 You mustn't be silly.
4 You must be polite.
5 You must wash your hands.
6 You must be quiet.
7 You mustn't listen to him.
8 You mustn't be late.
9 You must tidy your room.
10 You mustn't say that.

2
2 Don't be silly!   3 Be quiet!   4 Don't eat that!
5 Listen!   6 Don't sit down!

3
1 b   2 c   3 c   4 b   5 b

4
Check individual answers.

 At the moment

1
2 Final   3 billion   4 score   5 supporting
6 scarf   7 goal   8 all

2
2 f   3 e   4 g   5 d   6 b   7 a

3
eat: He's drawing, He's singing.
swim: He's sitting, He's getting up.
come: He's arguing, He's having lunch.

4
2 're/are supporting   3 're/are wearing
4 're/are sitting   5 's/is eating
6 's/is drinking   7 's/is standing

5
2 Who are you phoning? Rick.
3 Where's/Where is she going? To the swimming pool.
4 Why are they leaving? Because it's late.
5 Where's/Where is Sarah sitting? Next to Ben.
6 What are they watching? A programme about lions.
7 What's/What is the cat eating? Some fish.

6
Check individual answers.

1
2 He isn't reading. He is/'s looking at the spider.
3 I'm not working. I am/'m listening to music.
4 They aren't playing tennis. They are/'re arguing.
5 She isn't running. She is/'s having a drink.
6 They aren't playing. They are/'re sitting in the car.

2
2 Are you tidying your room? f
3 Am I dreaming? e
4 Are they arguing? b
5 Is Jack having his lunch? c
6 Is the film starting? a

3
1 They are/'re arguing. Yes, they are.
2 She is/'s having a shower. Yes, she is.
3 He is/'s watching a football match. No, he isn't.
4 They are/'re having breakfast. No, he isn't.

TAPESCRIPT
1   **A:** You're wearing my scarf!
     B: No, I'm not. This is my scarf.
     A: It isn't your scarf. It's my scarf!
     B: No, it's not!
2   *(singing in the shower)*
3   **BOY:** Come on, England!
4   **MRS KELLY:** Come on, Joe. You're late.
     JOE: OK. OK. Is there any toast?
     MRS KELLY: No, there isn't. Hurry up!

4
2 her   3 them   4 us   5 it   6 her   7 you   8 me

5
2 You aren't listening to me.
3 I love you.
4 Can you see him?
5 Don't interrupt me!
6 I never eat it.

6
Check individual answers.

1
2 raincoat   3 trousers   4 gloves   5 top   6 jeans
7 sunglasses   8 socks   9 jacket   10 coat
11 sandals   12 shorts

2
a   She is/'s wearing a dress, a jacket and shoes.
b   She wears jeans, a top and trainers.

3
Check individual answers.

 **Plans**

1
1 Tomorrow   2 Next month   3 Next year
4 at the weekend   4 next week   6 tonight

2
2 Tom is going to a party (at Sam's house).
3 Danny is watching football on TV.
4 Anna is having a piano lesson.
5 Helen's playing basketball (at the sports centre).

3
2 I'm playing volleyball tonight.
3 I'm not going to school tomorrow.
4 Are you staying at home this evening?
5 I'm visiting my grandparents at the weekend.
6 Are you going shopping on Saturday?

4
2 don't we watch a video?
3 play a computer game.
4 we go swimming?
5 listen to some music.
6 don't we go for a walk?

5
2 e   3 d   4 c   5 a   6 b

6
Check individual answers.

STEP 2

1
2 're/are going to see *The Lord of the Rings*.
3 's/is going to sit down.
4 's/is going to take a photo.
5 're/are going to have a pizza.
6 's/is going to buy the dress.

2
2 We aren't going to take any photos.
3 He isn't going to learn French.
4 They aren't going to stay in England.
5 She isn't going to see her friends.
6 I'm not going to wear my raincoat.

3
2 Are Mel's grandparents going to stay in England?
   No, they aren't.
3 Are they going to buy any postcards? Yes, they are.
4 Is Sadie going to see her friends this evening?
   No, she isn't.
5 Are you going to be a vegetarian?
   Yes, I am. / No, I'm not.

4
1 ✓   2 ✓   3 ✓   4 ✗   5 ✓   6 ✓   7 ✗   8 ✓

TAPESCRIPT

SADIE: Jack, what are you going to do in London?

JACK: I'm going to see the Tower of London.

SADIE: Are you going to visit the Natural History Museum?

JACK: Yes, I am. I want to see the blue whale.

SADIE: What about Buckingham Palace?

JACK: No, I'm not going to see Buckingham Palace. I'm not interested in that.

SADIE: What else are you going to do?

JACK: I'm going to look at the shops in Oxford Street.

SADIE: Are you going to buy anything?

JACK: Yes, I'm going to buy some new jeans.

SADIE: Where are you going to eat?

JACK: I'm not going to eat at a restaurant. I'm going to take some sandwiches.

5
1 c   2 c   3 a   4 a   5 b

6
Check individual answers.

STEP 3

1
2 It's raining in London.
3 It's snowing in Edinburgh.
4 It's windy in Exeter.
5 It's foggy in Birmingham.
6 It's sunny in Leeds.
7 It's cold in Edinburgh.

2
1 c   2 a   3 b   4 c   5 a   6 b

3
Check individual answers.

11 About the past

STEP 1

1
2 explorer   3 painter   4 writer   5 actor   6 scientist
7 footballer   8 actress

2
1 He was <u>in bed</u>.
2 <u>Where was</u> Sarah? <u>She wasn't</u> at school
   <u>She was in the river.</u>
3 <u>Where were</u> Pete and Sam? <u>They weren't</u> at school.
   They <u>were</u> at <u>the dentist/dentist's</u>.
4 <u>Where were</u> Mr and Mrs Carter? <u>They weren't</u> at work.
   <u>They were at the bus stop.</u>

3
1 B: were
2 A: Was   B: she wasn't; was
3 A: Was   B: he was; was
4 A: Were   B: they weren't; were
5 A: Were   B: I wasn't; was, [country]

4
There was a horse near the door.
There was a lamp by the window.
There was a coat on the floor.
There were two gloves on the table.
There was a black hat in the hall.
There were three small keys in a silver cup.
There was a silent clock on the wall.
There was a picture in my memory.
There was a happy, smiling face.
But there were empty chairs in every room.
And there were strange red lights in space.

5
2 There were some horses.
3 There was a train.
4 There weren't any football fans.
5 There was a baby.
6 There were some birds.
7 There was a bass guitar.
8 There were some dolphins.
9 There wasn't a piano.
10 There was a telephone.
11 There wasn't a clock.
12 There was a spaceship.

1530/-

6 Check individual answers.

1 b studied   c played   d saved   e arrived

1 played   2 lived   3 saved   4 studied
5 arrived   6 studied   7 saved   8 lived
9 played   10 arrived

2 started, appeared, stayed, arrived, travelled, followed, waited, listened, loved, changed, wanted

3 2 True.   3 True.   4 False.   5 False.   6 True.
7 True.   8 True.   9 False.   10 False.

4 2 c   3 g   4 f   5 h   6 a   7 b   8 e

5 *singer:* concert, voice
teacher: class, students, lesson
actor: Shakespeare, play, film
zoologist: binoculars, jungle, gorilla

1 2 Why did you open it?
3 Who did she phone?
5 Where did you find it?
6 What did you use?

2 2 Who did Sadie/she like?
3 What did Sadie/she hate?
4 What did Sadie/she prefer?
5 When did lessons start?
6 Where did the girls play?
7 When did school finish?
8 What did Sadie/she want to be?

3 Check individual answers.

12 Heroes

1 2 c   3 h   4 b   5 f   6 g   7 a   8 d

2 3 False. They didn't travel in spaceships.
4 False. He didn't play for Manchester United.
5 False. They weren't writers.
6 True.
7 False. He wasn't a member of the Beatles.
8 False. They didn't use mobile phones.

3 2 Did you watch television?
3 Did you clean your bike?
4 Did you wash your hair?
5 Did you tidy your room?
6 Did you phone Andy?

4 2 I didn't go to school last week.
3 I didn't play football at the weekend.
4 I was late for school yesterday morning.
5 Did you stay at home last night?

5 Check individual answers.

1
went	go	knew	know
came	come	had	have
saw	see	ate	eat
spoke	speak		

2 2 Where did he go? He went to the cinema.
3 What film did he see? He saw Dracula's Daughter.
4 What did he have at the café? He had a pizza.
5 What language did the woman speak?
She spoke Italian.
6 What time did Luke come home?
He came home at quarter past six.

3 1 b   2 b   3 b   4 a   5 b   6 a

TAPESCRIPT

SADIE: Where did you go?
JACK: We went to Paris.
SADIE: What was the weather like?
JACK: It was good. It was sunny.
SADIE: What did you do?
JACK: We visited the Louvre Museum.
And I went to the top of the Eiffel Tower.
SADIE: What was the food like?
JACK: It was OK. I just ate bread and cheese for lunch, and I usually had a pizza in the evening.
SADIE: Did you speak French?
JACK: Yes, I did. I spoke about three words – *Bonjour! Au revoir!* And *Merci!*

4 1 didn't go   2 knew   3 ate, didn't eat
4 didn't speak, spoke   5 saw, didn't see
6 went, didn't go

5 Check individual answers.

1 **Across**
1 photos   4 beach   6 USA   7 can   8 ship
9 train   10 sea   11 go   12 museum   13 postcards
Down
1 plane   2 ticket   3 sunglasses   4 ball
5 camping   10 shop   12 map

2 *Past:* d, h, i
Present: b, c, e, f
Future: g, h

3 Check individual answers.

Acknowledgements

The publishers are grateful to the following contributors:
Fran Banks: editorial work
Phil Burrows p.71, FLP pp.76, 83: illustrations.
pentacor**big**: text design and layouts